DESTINATION
SOUTHWEST

A Guide to
Retiring and Wintering in
Arizona, New Mexico
and Nevada

by
Michael Meyer and Sarah Muir

ORYX PRESS
1990

The rare Arabian Oryx is believed to have inspired the myth of the unicorn. This desert antelope became virtually extinct in the early 1960s. At that time several groups of international conservationists arranged to have 9 animals sent to the Phoenix Zoo to be the nucleus of a captive breeding herd. Today the Oryx population is nearly 800, and over 400 have been returned to reserves in the Middle East.

Copyright © 1990 by
The Oryx Press
2214 North Central at Encanto
Phoenix, Arizona 85004-1483

Cover Design: Terry Bliss

Published simultaneously in Canada

♾ The paper used in this publication meets the minimum requirements of American National Standard for Information Science—Permanence of Paper for Printed Library Materials, ANSI Z39.48, 1984.

The entries in this directory are based on subjective impressions gathered at the time when visits to the communities were made. Readers are cautioned to visit or phone to verify information listed because management or details about fees, amenities, or facilities may have changed.

Library of Congress Cataloging-in-Publication Data

Destination Southwest.

  1. Southwest, New—Description and travel—
1981- —Guide-books. 2. Retirement—Southwest,
New—Guide-books. 3. Moving, Household—Southwest,
New—Guide-books. I. Meyer, Michael, 1956, Dec. 6-
II. Muir, Sarah.
F787.D47 1990 917.904'33   90-7077
ISBN 0-89774-607-4

CONTENTS

INTRODUCTION

When we think of retirement, most of us picture sunny climates with lots of leisure activities. Our southwestern states offer plenty of both. It is our hope that this book will be of help to those people considering the Southwest as their retirement destination. We will take you to specific retirement developments throughout the area to give you a bird's-eye view of the variety of options available to you. Our reviews are based on personal visits to each location. With this information you will be able to determine which places you'll want to see for yourself and those that should be omitted. There is definitely something for everybody—as long as you do not ask for snowbound winters in the Southwest, so read on and be prepared to pack your bags!

HOW TO USE THIS BOOK

Destination Southwest includes the following sections:

- "Why the Southwest" is a lifestyle section, which provides an overview of the characteristics of the area, such as climate, types of housing, and recreational features, and gives you some idea of what to expect of the lifestyle once you are there.

- "Financial Considerations" is a section that gives you information on the financial intricacies of the very different types of facilities that are discussed and the questions to consider when making investments, such as renting vs buying or the value of amenities.

- Area reviews for cities or towns in Arizona, New Mexico, and Nevada are included for places that offer at least several retirement communities. Details of the general topics covered in the "Why the Southwest" section provide an even more complete picture of the specific area.

- Community reviews follow area reviews for each state and provide the following type of information for each retirement community:

  1. Independent Living Facility: describes the type of living situation and any assistance or care that may be offered.

  2. Housing Types Available: describes the types of units offered for sale or lease.

  3. Number of Sites: specifies the number of each type of unit in the community.

  4. Location: explains proximity to services and attractions and gives transportation requirements or provisions to access them.

  5. Requirements/Restrictions: specifies the age requirements for residents, for visitors, and whether pets are allowed.

  6. Fees: explains, in some detail, the costs of various units in a development and the extras that are offered for fees, such as greens fees for golf, fees for meals, utility fees, transportation, laundry, etc.

  7. Amenities: lists all of the features that are beyond the standard, such as pool and spa, activity rooms and their uses, meal plans, outings and trips, safety and care features, and others.

  8. Reviewer's Notes: A paragraph of comments from the author who visited the community, giving impressions from his/her perspective.

- Advertising, scattered through all of the sections, may be of interest or benefit to area newcomers.

One final note on the use of this book: Icons have been provided, in the upper left-hand corner of each community review, to help you to page through the volume and locate the communities that offer some of the features that are important to you before you even read the detailed entries. The following is a key to those icons, although most of them are self-explanatory:

❄ Indicates that provision is made for winter-visitor rentals

✋ Indicates that the community provides assisted-living services

🏠 Indicates a single-family dwelling

🏠 Indicates a duplex

🏢 Indicates a multi-family dwelling, including apartments, condominiums, or townhouses

🏬 Indicates a mobile-home community

🚐 Indicates an RV community

The cost information contained in this book has been checked for accuracy before publication. Please be aware that prices change and better deals can sometimes be negotiated. Do not be afraid to go after a more favorable financial arrangement, whether for a home or even a deposit on a rental property. These places want your business!

When you visit the communities featured please mention that you read about them in *Destination Southwest*. This well help to track usage and facilitate work on future books.

WHY THE SOUTHWEST?

CLIMATE

When recent newcomers are asked what their main reason was for choosing the Southwest as their new home, the answer most often given is the weather. Leaving harsh winters behind when it is time to retire has been part of the American Dream since the 1950s. The vast amount of inexpensive land available has enabled forward-thinking developers to create the active adult community concept. It has been 30 years since the first of these communities was established, and the idea is as popular as ever. Arizona leads the nation in numbers of adult communities, but her neighbors Nevada and New Mexico have begun to capitalize on similar natural resources.

The desert climate has long been thought of as more healthful for many ailments. Whether or not this is true, close to a million older people have chosen to relocate to desert areas. One serious problem with warm dry winters, however, is air pollution. During the winter months thermal air inversions trap dust and pollution in the valleys. Pollution from automobiles and industries is increasing every year. In areas subject to pollution, daily news reports advise people with respiratory conditions to stay indoors approximately 15 to 30 days each winter. The problem is confined for the most part to the Phoenix and Tucson areas (both cities are located in valleys). Outlying parts of both metropolitan areas have somewhat healthier air quality, however. In Phoenix these areas are Sun City, Mesa, Sun Lakes, and North Scottsdale. In Tucson the Green Valley area and northern developments have better air quality. It is always advisable to consult your physician if you are planning to move to an area with a different climate.

Summer monsoon storms usually appear in July and August. These storms, which almost always occur in the late afternoon and early evening, are characterized by sudden high winds, blowing dust, and thunderstorms with heavy rains. In desert areas high winds create dust storms that can severely limit visibility. If you are driving when one comes up, try to pull onto the shoulder of the road and put on your hazard lights. The storms are most often of short duration. Mountain areas receive more rain and less dust.

LIFESTYLE

The relaxed lifestyle of the Southwest is another enticement for retirees. The large cities function at a slower pace than their counterparts in the Midwest and East. Service industries are well staffed and long lines are infrequent. Traffic in Tucson and Phoenix can be quite frustrating, however. Rapid urban growth and the lack of public transportation make for heavy traffic on major arteries. A good thing about the highly developed popular retirement communities is that you will find almost everything you need without having to travel to highly congested areas. A car is almost a necessity in most of the largest and most popular active retirement communities. Where available, taxis and Dial-a-Ride can be obtained on a "call" basis. We did observe that there are a number of full-service and catered lifestyle facilities that are operating their own group transportation to necessary destinations. We have tried to indicate where this service is provided.

Casual clothing is acceptable at all but the toniest places. We have found that you have to look hard for very formal restaurants and night spots. Some of the country-club-type communities are a little less casual, but cruise/resort wear is always in style. Most natives and locals do not wear cowboy regalia, but blue jeans are a standard.

In the desert region there is very rarely occasion for a heavy coat, gloves, or a hat. If you are a first-time visitor a medium-weight, versatile jacket will suffice, even in the middle of winter. In Northern Arizona and New Mexico you should be prepared for more traditional winter weather, however.

HOUSING

Most of the available housing in the Southwest was built after 1960. Although there are exceptions, the majority of retiree housing has been developed in the last 30 years. Single-level homes predominate in this area and it is unusual to find basements. Building codes and standards vary from place to place, so it is always a good idea to have an independent contractor or inspection company check out homes that are more than 10 years old.

Heating systems operate either with electricity or natural gas; each type of system has its merits. Cooling systems—essential in the desert—are usually central refrigeration units. The "swamp" cooler or "evap" (evaporative) cooler is a type of system that uses circulating water and fans. Central refrigeration is the most effective system but is most expensive to operate. Evaporative coolers work well while humidity is low and consume far less electricity, but when the humidity starts climbing above 20 percent and outside temperatures are over 90 degrees, the swamp cooler creates exactly that atmosphere inside your home. Experts in this field say that having both types of cooling (they can operate through the same air ducts) provides the most cost-effective and comfortable system. Humidity does not usually go up until July and declines in the early part of September. Electric bills in Arizona range from an average of $200 a month for a fully-air-conditioned 1200-sq-ft home in the summer months to $50 to $60 per month in the winter for heating. This gives you a rough idea of what to expect. The figures can be reversed for the mountain areas, where winter heating is the primary cost.

RECREATION

The one thing the Southwest does not have is an ocean. Otherwise, from cactus-covered deserts to mountain ski resorts, the Southwest has it all. Outdoor activities take place year round. One great claim of Tucson, Arizona is that it is possible to swim in a heated backyard pool and drive from there to Mt. Lemmon's ski area within 45 minutes! Golf enthusiasts in desert areas are able to play comfortably all through the winter, and die-hard golfers are even visible on the greens when the temperature reaches 110 degrees.

Those who fish and boat will find numerous small lakes and large human-made reservoirs from which to choose. Lakes Mead and Powell are the two largest human-made reservoirs in the country. Both are formed from water from the Colorado River. Lake Mead alone has over 800 miles of shoreline and is over 100 miles long. It is located in Nevada and Arizona. The lake was created in 1935 when the 726-foot-high Hoover Dam was completed. It is a short drive from Las Vegas.

The slightly smaller, but scenically more striking Lake Powell is on the Utah/Arizona border. Contained by the Glen Canyon Dam, Lake Powell is world famous for its red rock canyons and the world's largest natural arch, Rainbow Bridge. The dam and Wahweap Marina are located right outside Page, Arizona.

Roosevelt, Apache, Canyon, Saguaro, Pleasant, and Bartlett lakes are also human-made. They provide Phoenix and the surrounding communities with their water supply as well as playing host to fans of water sports and fishing. Maximum travel time to any of these lakes is under two hours from anyplace in the metropolitan area.

FINANCIAL CONSIDERATIONS

Money considerations play an important part in every aspect of our lives, retirement being no exception. In fact, because this is a time of life when many people no longer are earning money and thus must live with a fixed income, the fear of financial ruin through unwise retirement decisions is significant. On the other hand, most of you who have reached this point in your life have learned through experience (the school of hard knocks) how to make major decisions correctly. Most people retiring or wintering in the Southwest will not be purchasing their first home; in fact it may be one in a series of several home purchases they have made. No matter what you read or hear, the basics are still valid (research, references, location). Rely on your past experience, and do not under any circumstances allow yourself to be convinced that because you are now retired you can no longer make the decisions that are right for *you*.

BUYING IN A RETIREMENT COMMUNITY

Although you may have a clear financial plan for your later years, it makes good sense to consult one of the available retirement planning guides, which can give you detailed approaches to budgeting various aspects of your retirement, including housing. A book we like is *Retiring Right* by Lawrence J. Kaplan, published by Avery Publishing Group, Wayne, New Jersey. Rather than duplicating the information these books provide, we will emphasize some of the more specific points to consider, based on our reviews of communities and developments in the Southwest. The following paragraphs offer a quick summary of the basics of retirement buying.

When buying in a retirement community, those of you with past experience will need to consider the same major criteria that prevailed when you bought your last home (your priorities will shift somewhat, however, if you are looking for assisted living or lifecare communities). These criteria are value, appreciation, size of house, and purchase price versus ongoing costs.

1. The components that make up value include basic price (you should definitely shop around); location; quality; and the value of amenities, both those offered as part of the development and those provided by the larger community.

2. To find out what the prospects for appreciation are, you need to know

- What similar houses in the area have sold for over the past five years.
- How hard it has been, and how long it has taken, to sell houses in this area.
- How stable the housing market is.
- How diversified the local economy is.
- How much new and competing housing is likely to be built in the area. (New and competing housing is a fairly major competitive threat to many retirees who bought in the Southwest 10 to 15 years ago, owing to the continuing availability of land for new construction.)

3. You need to consider what size house is appropriate for your needs and at the same time attractive to the resale market. For example, as a retiree, you would not necessarily be looking for a four-bedroom house; neither would most future buyers in a retirement community.

4. The relative value you place on purchase price versus ongoing costs should be carefully considered, and future increases should be taken into account. If you have a "nest egg" that allows you to purchase but relatively low ongoing retirement income, lower monthly costs in terms of mortgage payments, homeowners' fees, taxes, security, and so on will be more important to you than purchase price. Because costs are such an important part of your decision, we provide specific price ranges and fees for each development in our listings. The section entitled "Community Financial Packages" at the end of this section will assist you in analyzing and comparing options.

BUYING VERSUS RENTING

Many people feel comfortable only in their "own home." If you feel that way, renting will not seem an attractive option. However, there are certain benefits to renting, and a number of these benefits have increased in recent years. First, the overall quality of the rental market has improved—we were impressed with the rental communities we reviewed—and your options have significantly increased. Secondly, the tax advantages of home ownership have decreased. Finally, renting gives you greater mobility. The following guidelines may help you decide whether to buy or rent.

Buy if you

- Know the area well and are comfortable with it.
- Plan to stay at least five years.
- Want your own home.
- Are in a stable housing market.
- Like the amenities offered.
- See potential for appreciation.

Rent if you

- Do not know the area or are not sure whether it is right for you.
- May move in the near future.
- Do not see much appreciation in the market.
- Can get the amenities you want in the rental market.

THE VALUE OF AMENITIES AND SERVICES OFFERED

You will find that amenities abound in retirement communities, all of which seek to serve the lifestyles they perceive you desire. Many communities include these amenities as part of ongoing homeowners' fees or monthly rental fees; others do not. A good way to evaluate the "true value" of these amenities is to determine locally what the amenity would cost if you were purchasing it from an outside vendor. Call local suppliers and ask what they would charge you to provide a service such as lawn care or security at your home. When renting (less often with a purchase) you can frequently negotiate a lesser fee if there are certain amenities you do not want (such as meal service).

Described below are the amenities and services we have encountered:

Security: Many communities stress the importance of security, depending on their location. Leisure World, located in urban Mesa, stresses its security features which include a 24-hour guarded gate house and a security patrol—services you pay for in your monthly fees. On the other hand, more isolated Sun City and Green Valley use volunteers to staff their security patrols, there are no fees, and crime rates are very low.

Lawn Service: Most communities include in their homeowner's fees basic charges for maintenance of common areas, streets, and landscaping—but not your own individual lots. Most of the townhouse communities will include a more complete lawn service. Usually we are talking about desert landscaping, which requires very little care compared with lawn and garden maintenance needed in other climates.

Nurse on Call: Some communities provide for 24-hour nurse on call and/or emergency call services installed in your home. These medical emergency services tend to be very basic or nonexistent in active retirement communities and become more sophisticated in assisted living environments.

Utilities, Water, Sewer Usage, Trash Collection, and Fire Protection: These services are not usually included in the basic homeowners' fees so you should get estimates as to individual costs on these items.

Recreational Amenities: Most communities include use of all community and recreational amenities as part of their homeowners' or rental fees. Usually not included, however, is the daily golf fee. Some communities have private courses that allow only homeowners and guests access; others are public. If this is important to you be sure to check carefully.

Community recreational buildings range from large, elegant clubhouses with a country-club atmosphere to smaller block type centers oriented to clubs and art and handicrafts. Amenities include swimming pools, tennis, shuffleboard, exercise, art and handicrafts, cards, billiards, library, banquet rooms, and virtually any other activity imaginable.

QUESTIONS TO CONSIDER

A number of other questions arose during visits to retirement communities. A few have significant financial consequences that we would like to point out.

1. Unincorporated Areas: A number of these communities (including some of the oldest and best regarded, such as Sun City) are in unincorporated areas. This means that taxes, police, fire protection, and certain other issues can change or be greatly affected by county policies. Do not assume that a marketing address of "Phoenix" or "Tucson" means that the community is in an incorporated area.

2. Pre-retirement Purchase Plans: A number of communities have plans that allow you to buy either your lot, or house and lot, ahead of time and then move one to two years later in order to give you time to sell your home. These deals can be good or bad depending upon your situation and the "fine" print. For example what happens if you cannot sell the home you currently occupy within that time frame? Plans that allow you to buy only your lot may be better in this circumstance.

3. Start-up Developments: Be careful when buying or renting in a start-up development. This is especially true if you are older and/or not prepared to hold a long-term investment. We visited one start-up development that had gone out of business after completing 12 houses and the clubhouse.

ASSISTED LIVING

Our investigation of retirement communities indicated that "assisted living" means different things to different people. For an active couple just retiring, when one member of the family has some limitations, it can mean basic housing design issues such as single-level housing, flat landscaping, wide corridors and doors, lower shelves/cabinets, and walk-in showers or low bathtubs. For other people it can mean meal service, housekeeping, and transportation services; and for others it may mean nursing staff or nurses' aides located on premise to provide assistance in daily living.

A good working definition of assisted living is a community environment that provides both custodial services (such as housekeeping and meals) and nursing/nurses' aides assistance (such as assistance in taking medicine), as well as certain other daily needs, but not the 24-hour care a person would receive in a nursing facility.

The term "catered living" and "personal care" are often used in place of assisted living. "Congregate care" is also used to describe assisted living, but in this case the emphasis is on common services such as meals in a community setting. "Personal care" is also a term used by medical professionals in describing services provided by a nursing facility.

From a financial standpoint, if you are buying, many of these assisted living amenities are included in monthly fees. In addition, if you are buying a new home, you can often plan for a custom design that will accommodate your needs. In rental situations some communities may offer these amenities as optional, while others require you to take them.

Amenity Levels in Assisted Living Communities

Basic Design	Single-level housing, flat landscaping, wide corridors and doors, and walk-in showers or low bathtubs.
Catered and Custodial	Housekeeping services, shared meal/common dining service, transportation services, organized activities, reception desk.
Personal and Medical	Medical emergency call buttons in baths and bedrooms, guardrail in bath, guardrail in corridors, nursing staff on premise, personnel to assist with in-home personal care and medical needs.

LIFECARE COMMUNITIES

The basic concept of the lifecare community is to combine a person's current and future housing and medical needs within one community. The retiree pays certain entrance and monthly fees in return for certain guarantees and possible refunds. Refunds are usually based on certain formulas and contingent upon resale of the unit. Lifecare may be very appropriate for someone who is isolated, still healthy, but has some medical problems that affect independence. The reputation and prior experience of the developer/owner is very important, and caution is advised if you are looking at a community where less than 50 percent of the housing has been sold. Fees range widely in these communities depending upon a lot of factors. In the Southwest typical entrance fees range from $50,000 to $125,000 with monthly fees in the $900 to $2000 range.

Buying into such a community is far more complicated than the other options discussed in our book and definitely requires the advice of professionals. There is information available strictly on this topic. One brochure we like is *Continuing Care Retirement Community* published by the American Association of Homes for the Aging, Washington, D.C. Another good reference is an article entitled "What to Look for in Life Care" by Marie Hodge, *50 Plus Magazine*, July 1988. What makes the transaction complicated is that you are making certain contractual commitments and seeking guarantees for your future. Some states, including Arizona, have much stronger licensing and other regulatory requirements for these communities than for rental communities.

GOVERNMENT SUBSIDIZED HOUSING (HUD) RETIREMENT COMMUNITIES

A number of rental retirement communities offer rent subsidy for people who are 62 and older, and/or handicapped, and meet certain federally mandated criteria for housing. Highest priority is given to persons categorized as those who are involuntarily displaced, living in substandard housing, or paying in excess of 50 percent of their income in rent. Many subsidized housing communities provide only subsidized housing and because demand exceeds supply only persons who fall in the highest priority category get apartments. Some, like Glencroft in the Phoenix area, have a portion of their housing designated as subsidized.

Rent, on a subsidized basis, is usually 30 percent of the adjusted income of the resident. Potential residents are required to fill out an application indicating information on income and medical history.

In the course of this book we visited a number of these communities (such as Encino House East in Albuquerque and Glencroft) and were impressed by many.

COMMUNITY FINANCIAL PACKAGES

As you will see from our reviews, not only are there great variations in the types of communities you may choose, but there are also a multitude of options and features available within each community.

We have prepared eight sample financial packages to assist you in analyzing and comparing these options. Each sample is taken from a major type of community we visited. Financial information is based on information provided by the community for a residence occupied by two people. Since prices vary greatly—some are a lot higher or lower than the samples—no option should be ruled out because the sample appears either too pricey or too cheap. Our individual reviews provide specific prices that will help you more in that regard.

The eight samples that follow are: traditional rental, winter-visitor rental, recreational vehicle community rental, catered or assisted living rental, traditional home purchase, townhouse/condominium purchase, traditional manufactured home purchase, and lifecare community.

1. TRADITIONAL RENTAL

- Monthly rent, one bedroom, unfurnished $ 625.00
- Additional person charge[1]   50.00
- Utilities[2] (extra charge)   ?
- Basic telephone/cable TV   30.00
- Covered parking   15.00

TOTAL MONTHLY $ 720.00

SOURCE: Royal Palms, Mesa, Arizona

2. TRADITIONAL WINTER-VISITOR RENTAL

- Monthly rent, one bedroom, furnished $ 1,305.00
- Additional person charge   50.00
- Utilities[2] (extra charge)   ?
- Basic telephone[3] (extra charge)   ?
- Covered parking   15.00

TOTAL MONTHLY $ 1,370.00

SOURCE: Royal Palms, Mesa, Arizona

---

1. An Additional person charge for the second person in an apartment is not uncommon in the Southwest.

2. Often included. If not, utilities can run $200 a month in the summer for air conditioning. Some communities (such as Royal Palms) provide a utility allowance.

3. Basic telephone and cable TV are often included as part of furnished apartment rentals. You pay for long distance calls, however.

3. RECREATION VEHICLE COMMUNITY

- Monthly lot rental[4] $ 325.00

  plus tax

- Water and Sewer (included)   —
- Trash (included)   —
- Security (included)   —
- Utilities (extra charge)   ?
- Telephone and cable TV   30.00

TOTAL -

PLUS UTILITIES/TAXES   355.00

SOURCE: Sunflower Resort, Surprise, Arizona

4. CATERED/ASSISTED LIVING

RENTAL

- Monthly rent, one bedroom, unfurnished $ 975.00
- Additional person charge   300.00
- Housekeeping/maid service[5] (included)   —
- Scheduled transportation[6] (included)   —
- Meals[7] (included)   —
- Utilities[8] (included)   —
- Basic telephone/cable TV   30.00
- Covered parking   15.00

TOTAL MONTHLY $ 1,320.00

SOURCE: The Fountains at La Cholla, Tucson, Arizona

---

4. RV communities allow residents to rent daily, weekly, monthly, or yearly. Typical rates are daily, $18; weekly, $108 plus tax (electric included); yearly, $1375-$1625 plus tax (plus electric). Purchase of recreational vehicles runs from $2000 for a small travel trailer to $100,000 for a deluxe motor home.

5. Usually every other week; sometimes weekly.

6. Most communities have mini-vans or buses which take residents shopping or to doctor's appointments.

7. Usually one main meal per day (either lunch or dinner) and a continental breakfast. Many variations are available.

8. Typically (included).

5. TRADITIONAL RETIREMENT COMMUNITY HOME PURCHASE

Initial

- 2 bedroom, 2 bath with carport — $103,495
- Home site/lot[9] (included) — —
- Custom design costs[10] (extra charge) — ?

TOTAL — $103,495

Ongoing Monthly

- Homeowner fees[11] — $ 25
- Recreation association fees[12] — —
- Golf fees (extra charge) — ?
- Taxes[13] — 80
- Utilities[14] (extra charge) — ?
- Water — 15
- Sewer — 5
- Trash — 10
- Telephone and cable — 30

TOTAL PLUS UTILITIES — $ 165

SOURCE: Sun Lakes, Sun Lakes, Arizona

6. TOWNHOUSE/CONDOMINIUM

Initial

- One bedroom, one and a half baths[15] — $ 65,500
- Custom design costs[10] (extra charge) — ?

TOTAL — $ 65,500

Ongoing Monthly

- Homeowner/condominium fees[16] — $ 216
- Utilities (included) — —
- Water and sewer (included) — —
- Trash (included) — —
- Landscaping/lawn maintenance (included) — —
- Assisted living services[17] (extra charge) — ?
- Telephone and cable TV — 30
- Taxes — 31

TOTAL — $ 277

SOURCE: Scottsdale Shadows, Scottsdale, Arizona

---

9. The cost of a standard home site/lot is often included in the home purchase price. Special or larger lots cost more. Some options allow pre-purchase of the lot or home.

10. Include custom changes to your home (walls, bathrooms, etc.), additional features (pool), and landscaping. Costs vary depending on what you can negotiate.

11. Homeowner association fees include maintenance of common community areas (roads, landscaping) and security. Often they also include fees for all recreation services (usually not golf), and sometimes water, sewer, and trash services. *Be careful to check what is included here—there are a lot of variations.*

12. Recreation fees, except golf membership, are usually included in homeowner fees. There usually is a daily fee to play.

13. Vary depending on local area; generally much lower than east/midwest.

14. Vary depending on the area. If there are resales in the area, check with the local utility as to average monthly bills. Consider also installation of a swamp cooler. Utility bills in the summer run $300 per month.

15. A large number of variations fit this category including duplexes, townhouses, and apartments in high rise buildings.

16. Homeowner association fees are typically higher and may include more basic services (for example, utilities) than association fees in traditional home developments.

17. Some communities offer assisted living services; monthly charges then are in the $500 range.

7. TRADITIONAL MANUFACTURED HOME

Initial

- Manufactured home, two bedroom, two bath — $ 30,000
- Installation on lot, custom design[18] — 7,500

TOTAL — $ 37,500

Ongoing Monthly

- Residential space rent[19] — $ 250
- Water and sewer (included) — —
- Trash (included) — —
- Security (included) — —
- Utilities (extra charge) — ?
- Telephone and cable TV — 30

TOTAL — $ 280

SOURCE: Paradise Peak West, Phoenix, Arizona

8. LIFECARE COMMUNITY

Initial

- One bedroom apartment[20] — $ 98,500

TOTAL — $ 98,500

Ongoing Monthly

- Monthly fees — $ 875
- Additional person charge — 450
- Housekeeping/maid service (included) — —
- Meals (included) — —
- Utilities (included) — —
- Scheduled transportation (included)
- Basic telephone and cable TV — 30
- Nursing home fees[21] (included)

TOTAL — $ 1,355

SOURCE: The Forum · Pueblo Norte, Scottsdale, Arizona

---

18. Typically you purchase a new home from one of a number of dealers and then have it installed on the lot of your choice. Installation usually includes all hookups, setup on lot, carport, construction of cover around the home, and any custom design. Resales are also available.

19. Other communities sell lots with homes and charge homeowner association fees similar to any other housing development.

20. Initial membership, endowment or buy-in fee that entitles resident to assisted living services and certain guarantees for future housing and nursing home services if needed.

21. In the event a resident requires nursing home care, they are guaranteed a space and the cost charged to them either is the monthly fee or some other formula but significantly less than normal home costs.

If you're tired of clipping the hedges, try clipping this coupon.

Yard work. House work. Car repairs. Retirement shouldn't mean more time to do your chores, it should mean more time away from them.

That's why you should con-sider life at a Hillhaven Retirement Community. Every Hillhaven community offers all kinds of extras, in a uniquely affordable setting. So instead of clipping the hedges, clip this coupon instead.

Valley Manor
Tucson, Arizona
(602) 886-7937

Villa Campana
Tucson, Arizona
1-800-729-0007

Campana del Rio
Tucson, Arizona
(602) 299-1941

Olive Grove
Phoenix, Arizona
1-800-842-4785

Kachina Point
Sedona, Arizona
(602) 284-1021

TELL ME MORE ABOUT HILLHAVEN COMMUNITIES
I have checked the Hillhaven community that interests me most. Please send me information as soon as possible.

☐ Olive Grove   ☐ Kachina Point   ☐ Valley Manor

☐ Campana del Rio   ☐ Villa Campana

Name _____

Address _____

City _____ State _____ Zip _____

Phone _____

Please return this coupon to: The Hillhaven Corporation • 1550 E. River Road • Tucson, AZ 85718 • ATTN: Susan Roos

ARIZONA

BULLHEAD CITY, AZ/LAUGHLIN, NV

Bullhead City and Laughlin lie on either side of the Colorado River at the southernmost tip of Nevada bordering Arizona. There is a bridge linking the two cities, as well as ferry service provided by Laughlin's casinos. While Laughlin provides 24-hour-a-day action at the casinos, Bullhead City in Arizona supplies most of the residential housing. This is said to be the fastest growing area in Arizona.

The warm, dry climate in addition to the water sports and gambling casinos attract many visitors, especially in the winter. Average temperatures in July range from 108.2 to 79.1 degrees; in January from 62.2 to 44.8 degrees. Average yearly rainfall is 4.19 inches. The population is approximately 25,000, up from 10,363 in 1980. The main economic activities in the area are tourism, hydroelectric generators, and the eight casinos on the Nevada side.

Recreational facilities include fishing and water sports on the Colorado River and nearby Mohave and Mead lakes, casino gambling and shows, and golf at Chaparral Country Club. The Black Mountain Range to the east is interesting for hiking, taking photographs, exploring old ghost towns, and hunting.

This area is located about 230 miles from Phoenix and 90 miles from Las Vegas. As with most towns on the Colorado River, there are numerous RV parks for winter visitors (21 parks with a total of 2463 sites). Property owners in Bullhead City pay $10.62 per

$100 assessed valuation. Nevada residents pay no state income tax, which is a plus to many retirees.

Services in the area include one hospital, one extended care facility, over 35 physicians and dentists, several banks and savings and loans, and shopping. There is also a small airport that handles regional direct carriers as well as private planes. For further information contact: Bullhead Area Chamber of Commerce, PO Box 66, Bullhead City, AZ 86430, or call (602) 754-4121.

MESA, AZ

Located in the Phoenix metropolitan area to the east of Phoenix, Scottsdale, and Tempe, Mesa is Arizona's third largest city. In 1988 the population was 269,440 (almost doubled since 1980). However, in the last year or so growth appears to have slowed, based on the number of new building permits issued. Winter visitors boost the population to an estimated 450,000+ during the winter months.

Mesa has long been recognized as a good place to retire. The first retirement communities here were established in the late 1950s, and new development has been continuous since then. RV and mobile home parks, apartment rentals, and motel rooms are available on a seasonal basis. RV spaces with full hookups number around 30,000, and there are approximately 4000 hotel and motel rooms. As a city, Mesa has a tradition of being family oriented and boasts a top-rated school system in addition to its

numerous facilities for retirees. Property taxes in 1988 were $9.82 per $100 of assessed valued.

Health care services in Mesa include four hospitals with a total of 950 beds, over 400 physicians, 200 dentists and 18 convalescent homes.

Community and recreation facilities include three libraries, the Mesa Symphony, the Mormon Temple, several historical museums, a civic center, 40 parks, 20 golf courses (public and private), and over 100 tennis courts. Mesa is also home to the Chicago Cubs and California Angels during spring training. Other teams have camps in the area so baseball fans can enjoy games in the early spring when the average temperature is around 75 degrees.

For more information on Mesa, contact the Mesa Chamber of Commerce, 120 North Center Street, Mesa, AZ 85201, (602) 969-1307, or the Mesa-Chandler-Tempe Board of Realtors, PO Box 5139, Mesa, AZ 85211.

PHOENIX, GLENDALE, AND TEMPE, AZ

Greater Phoenix includes Mesa, Scottsdale, Chandler, Paradise Valley, Peoria, Glendale, Tempe, Sun Cities, and other smaller communities in the "Valley of the Sun." It is one of the 10 largest metropolitan areas in the country. (Mesa, Scottsdale, Paradise Valley, and Sun Cities are each given separate reviews, which the reader should refer to for specifics on those areas.) The period of high growth experienced by this area in the late 1970s and early 1980s has tapered off, leaving the real estate market flooded and very competitive. The area offers just about all one could expect of a large city. There is a busy international airport (Sky Harbor), full-time symphony orchestra, renowned medical

facilities, and so forth. One problem is transportation. Freeways and roads are not adequate to handle the large volume of cars. Public transportation is not well used nor is it very convenient.

The valley offers a hot dry climate with a two-hour drive to snow and mountains. Average January temperatures range from 64 to 38 degrees. July averages are 105 to 78 degrees. Pollution can be a problem during the winter months. Persons with respiratory problems should consult a physician before considering a lengthy stay.

Glendale, located to the north and west of Phoenix, has a population of about 123,000. Founded in the late 1800s, it was primarily a farming town until urbanization began. Today it is a mixture of industrial, commercial, and residential properties. Retirees find the northwestern area of Glendale attractive because of its proximity to the Sun Cities area. Property taxes run about $9.20 per $100 assessed valuation.

Tempe is located east of Phoenix and is the home of Arizona State University. ASU has an enrollment of well over 35,000 students, many of whom live off-campus in Tempe. The total population is 150,000. Tempe is mainly residential with several industrial parks in its southwestern area. The Arizona State University stadium is also home to the Phoenix Cardinals football team, formerly of St. Louis. Most of the cultural life in the community revolves around the university.

QUARTZSITE, AZ

Remember Woodstock? Well picture a place in the middle of the desert about as far away from any place as you can imagine. Add more than 1,000,000 people, most from the same generation and make rock—that is, *rocks*—the focal point. What you have is the annual Quartzsite Pow Wow gem show... The Woodstock for retirees.

Quartzsite is located on Interstate 10 about 30 miles from the California border—a town that until recently had a summertime population that hovered around 100—lower than the average daytime temperature during those months. However, progress reached Quartzsite in 1989 and the town is now incorporated with some 1500 residents.

February 1991 will mark the 25th annual Pow Wow and again hundreds of thousands of rockhounds and RVers will flock to the area. The average length of stay is two weeks, but an estimated 10,000 stay until April. There are only three small motels in town so almost everyone brings a motorhome, travel trailer, van, or even tent and searches for a spot close to the action. The Bureau of Land Management (BLM) permits RVs to stay free

on public land for up to two weeks ($25 for a stay up to six months). There are several recognized campgrounds, but very few have full hookups or modern amenities. Self-contained vehicles are necessary for a comfortable stay. There is adequate refuse clean-up and "dump stations" are provided to keep the area clean and sanitary. In addition to the gem show (many visitors never see it), there is an unofficial gigantic "swap meet" or tag sale. Thousands of people bring things to sell or trade, everything from fine handcrafted jewelry to Taiwanese treasures to household castoffs. Everyone is there to have a good time, meet new people, and escape cold weather. Many people we spoke with go annually and would not miss it. They say they were skeptical before their first trip but now they are addicted. Aside from the serious rockhounds, 25% there are retirees. Security is not reported to be a problem in spite of the huge crowd.

For more information you can contact the Quartzsite Chamber of Commerce. Reservations need to be made about a year in advance for motel rooms and the few "full hookup" RV spaces. However, the BLM has yet to run out of space and that is where you will find most of the regular visitors. There are several small grocery stores in town but Blythe, California is only 30 miles away and has many well-stocked supermarkets and other essential services. To quote one annual visitor: "Try it, you'll like it." Contact the Quartzsite Chamber of Commerce, PO Box 85, Quartzsite, AZ 85346, (602) 927-5600; or Bureau of Land Management.

SCOTTSDALE, PARADISE VALLEY, AND CAREFREE, AZ

Located north and east of Phoenix, these three communities are part of the Phoenix metropolitan area. They are considered by some to be the more prestigious communities in the area. Strict zoning laws are enforced to keep an "affluent" appearance. Large homes in the southwestern style prevail.

Scottsdale has a population of approximately 120,000. Its population is diverse, with many families (there is a good school system) and a number of retirement facilities. There are several hospitals as well as the new Mayo Clinic. There is no lack of places to to shop—choices range from discount stores to designer boutiques. Many of the Valley's famous resorts are located here, as well as many fine restaurants. The climate is the same as in Phoenix and is therefore ideal for year-round outdoor activities. Property taxes per $100 assessed valuation are under $9.

The town of Paradise Valley is located in northeast Phoenix, to the east of Scottsdale. Its boundaries are not well defined. The community encompasses mountain areas with fabulous homes and estates. Real estate values are quite high and homes must be at least 2000 sq ft by town ordinance. Paradise Valley's location makes all of the valley easily accessible. "Paradise Valley" can also refer to a larger general area of Phoenix; the same strict zoning requirements do not apply.

Carefree is just north of Scottsdale. Planned development began in 1960. There are small hills with large boulders throughout the community and the homes have been designed to "fit in" with the natural landscape. Because it lies 1000 feet higher than Phoenix, temperatures are somewhat cooler—usually about 5 degrees. Carefree has approximately 3000 residents, many of whom are celebrities. There are some townhouses being developed, but in most cases homes are for resale or built new on vacant property. Again, strict zoning applies for new construction.

For more information on the greater Phoenix metropolitan area contact the following sources: Carefree Chamber of Commerce, PO Box 734, Carefree, AZ 85377. Greater Paradise Valley Chamber of Commerce, 16042 N 32nd Street, #D-17, Phoenix, AZ 85032, (602) 482-3341. Scottsdale Chamber of Commerce, 7333 Scottsdale Mall, PO Box 130, Scottsdale, AZ 85252, (602) 945-8481.

SEDONA, COTTONWOOD, CAMP VERDE, AND JEROME, AZ

Geographically very near, the towns of Sedona, Cottonwood, Camp Verde, and Jerome each have different characteristics that make them unique. This area is called the Verde Valley, but Sedona is more likely to fall into its own special category of "red rock country." Located in the geographical center of Arizona about 100 miles north of Phoenix, Verde Valley offers cooler temperatures and wonderful scenic attractions. Although there are few retirement developments, the area has one of the highest proportions of retired individuals in the state. A wide price range of homes exists in the area, with Sedona being the most expensive and Camp Verde the least. Jerome, a mining boom town in the late 1800s and early 1900s, became a ghost town until the 1960s, when various artists reclaimed it. It is still home to many talented artists, but housing is in very short supply.

Cottonwood and Camp Verde are at an elevation of 3100 feet and experience a mild four season climate. Average January temperatures range from 57 to 29 degrees. There are a few inches of snow each winter which melt quickly, and the average rainfall is around 15 inches. It is worth mentioning that allergy sufferers in these two cities sometimes have problems in all but the winter months. Camp Verde's population is approximately 5800 and Cottonwood's around 6500. Both cities continue to grow. The area is served by a 96-bed hospital in Cottonwood. All services are available in the area.

Sedona is located in beautiful Oak Creek Canyon. Many visitors favorably compare this area with the Grand Canyon. Artists of all types work and maintain galleries here, and shopping in the many boutiques can yield many interesting and unique finds. Homes and home sites are expensive and in fairly short supply. Sedona's population in 1988 was 10,260. The elevation is 4300 feet, and the climate is again mild throughout the four seasons. Average temperatures in January are 55 to 30 degrees. July averages are 95 to 65 degrees. There is an average snowfall of around 9 inches and rainfall of about 17 inches.

There are many points of interest in the area. Jerome has maintained the look of the old west and has many interesting shops. Sedona has many galleries and resorts. Worth seeing is the Tlaquepaque "shopping center," styled after an old Mexican village. It has won many architectural awards and is truly unique.

Average prices for resale homes are: Camp Verde, $40,000; Cottonwood, $50,000; and Sedona, $90,000. Property taxes in these areas are between $10 and $13 per $100 assessed valuation. For further information contact: Verde Valley Chamber of Commerce, 1010 South Main Street, Cottonwood, AZ 86326 (602) 634-7593. Sedona Chamber of Commerce, PO Box 478, Sedona, AZ 86336 (602) 282-7722.

SUN CITY, SUN CITY WEST, AND YOUNGTOWN, AZ

Sun City, Sun City West, and Youngtown are located northwest of Phoenix and are considered part of the Phoenix metropolitan area. These three cities are comprised almost entirely of adults (Youngtown does have a few families with children). Because of the nature of the population, all the necessary components for retirement are provided. In addition to the large number of recreational activities available, the area is well supplied with health care facilities devoted to the older segment of the population. Civic organizations are numerous and there is great civic pride due to the homogeneous population.

The combined population was 62,288 in 1988. For the same year property tax rates were as follows: Sun City, $8.74 per $100 assessed valuation; Sun City West, $9.00; and Youngtown, $10.41.

Average temperatures for January range from 66 degrees to 35 degrees and for July, 106.3 degrees to 74.7 degrees. Average annual precipitation is 7.65 inches.

For more information, contact the Northwest Valley Chamber of Commerce, PO Box 5, Sun City, AZ 85372, or call (602) 583-0692.

TUCSON, AZ

Tucson is the second largest city in Arizona, with a population of over 350,000. It is located about two hours southeast of Phoenix and has a slightly cooler average temperature. It was established in 1775 by Spanish missionaries and is still referred to as the Old Pueblo. It has a diverse mix of residents due to its proximity to Mexico and the fact that it is a college town. It also has a more quaint and less urban feeling than its more metropolitan sister city of Phoenix. For example, most main streets in Tucson do not have sidewalks. Traffic congestion is a problem at times in the city. Cultural and artistic activities are more popular than in Phoenix—a point of pride for many of the residents. Tucson has been a favorite choice among retirees for many years. Green Valley, a retirement community 25 miles south of Tucson, just celebrated its 25th anniversary. Tucson has excellent health services and extensive community and recreational facilities. Property taxes were $12.97 per $100 assessed valuation in 1988.

Average temperatures for January range from 66 degrees to 37 degrees and for July, 101 degrees to 73 degrees. Average annual precipitation is 10.73 inches and it does on occasion snow in Tucson.

For more information on Tucson, contact the Tucson Metropolitan Chamber of Commerce, 465 West St. Mary's Road, PO Box 3028, Tucson, AZ 85702, or call (602) 792-1212.

YUMA, AZ

Yuma is located in the extreme southwest corner of Arizona, in the delta area of the Colorado and Gila Rivers, and was incorporated in 1871. Historically, Yuma has been important as the site of a sixteenth-century Spanish mission, a territorial prison, and Fort Yuma. Yuma served as a port in the late 1800s for steamboats shipping goods from the Pacific Coast via the Gulf of California and on up the Colorado River. The damming of the river now prohibits this.

Mild winters and hot dry summers are common in Yuma. Average temperatures in July range from 106.6 to 73.6 degrees; January temperatures average 68.4 to 36.8 degrees. Annual rainfall is low, averaging 2.99 inches. The population in 1988 was 50,755. Yuma continues to grow at a moderate rate.

The economy is dominated by agriculture and tourism. Unemployment is higher than the average at over 15 percent. Median home value is around $66,000, and property tax averages about $13.50 per $100 assessed valuation.

Yuma lies 183 miles from Phoenix, 174 miles from San Diego and 311 miles from Las Vegas. It is 20 miles from the Mexican border. All services are located within the city limits.

There is a 283-bed regional medical center, and nearly 200 physicians practicing in the area. A regional airport has flights daily to and from Phoenix and Los Angeles. Recreational facilities include four golf courses, 15 tennis courts, an adult center, movie theaters, and eight parks.

Yuma's climate is very attractive to winter visitors, and there are many RV and mobile home parks to accommodate the large seasonal influx. We have compiled a partial listing of these facilities, with phone numbers and number of spaces (all those listed have full hookups). For more information contact: Yuma County Chamber of Commerce, Box 230, Yuma, AZ 85364, (602) 782-2567.

Araby Acres, (602) 344-8666, 338 RV spaces.

Atlasta Trailer Park, (602) 783-1925, 20 mobile home spaces, 88 RV spaces.

Bonita Mesa RV Park, (602) 342-2999, 535 RV spaces.

Cactus Garden RV Park, (602) 342-9188, 242 RV spaces.

Capri Mobile Park, (602) 726-0959, 97 mobile home spaces, 207 RV spaces.

Cocopah Bend RV Resort, (602) 343-9300, 806 RV spaces.

Country Roads RV Village, (602) 344-8910, 1300 RV spaces.

Desert Palms Mobile Home Park, (602) 344-1016, 84 mobile home spaces.

Desert Paradise RV Resort, (602) 342-9313, 234 RV spaces.

Fortuna de Oro RV Park, (602) 342-5051, 226 RV Spaces.

Hidden Cove Park & Marina, (602) 783-3534, 40 mobile home spaces, 65 RV spaces.

Martinez Lake Resort, (602) 783-0253.

May Avenue Park, (602) 783-0883, 114 mobile home spaces, 30 RV spaces.

Mesa Verde RV Park, (602) 726-5814, 83 mobile home spaces, 30 RV spaces.

Oasis Gardens Adult RV Park, (602) 782-2222, 148 RV spaces.

Riverfront RV Park, (602) 783-5868.

Roger's RV Resort (602) 342-2992, 720 RV spaces.

Shady Acres Mobile Home and RV Park, (602) 783-9431, 81 mobile home spaces, 79 RV spaces.

Shangri-La RV Park, (602) 342-9123, 302 RV spaces.

Sundance RV Park, (602)342-9333, 503 RV spaces.

Sun Vista RV Resort, (602)726-8920, 1230 RV spaces.

Town and Country Adult Mobile Home Park, (602) 726-9512, 40 furnished mobile home rentals, 4 RV spaces.

Villa Alameda RV Park, (602) 344-8081, 302 RV spaces.

Yuma Home Park, (602) 344-2733, 95 mobile homes for rent.

Yuma Venture RV, (602) 342-9592, 140 RV spaces.

RIVERVIEW RV RESORT

2000 East Ramar Road

Bullhead City, AZ 86442

(602) 763-5800

INDEPENDENT LIVING FACILITY

An adults-only RV park with a nine-hole executive golf course. Established in 1984, owned and managed by R.C. Roberts & Company.

HOUSING TYPES AVAILABLE

Only class I RVs that are self-contained are permitted on rented space. Any RV over 10 years old is subject to approval by the management. Spaces have full hookups and cable TV is available.

NUMBER OF SITES/UNITS

697 RV spaces.

LOCATION

Bullhead City is located on the Arizona side of the Colorado River. Laughlin, Nevada, on the opposite bank, offers numerous gambling casinos. Riverview RV Resort is very near a hospital, doctors' offices, shopping, and other services. Mild winters, many RV resorts, inexpensive meals at casinos, and gambling make this area a haven for retirees.

REQUIREMENTS/RESTRICTIONS

Adults only. Small pets are welcome.

FEES

Four different rates are available: daily, weekly, monthly, and full season (six months). The daily rate is $14.75 and includes electricity and cable TV reception. The weekly rate, $88.50, includes electricity and cable TV. The monthly rate, $240, does not include electricity or cable TV. The full season rate is $1250 without electricity or cable TV. Golf course rates (nine hole) for residents are $6 daily; $7 for nonresidents. Monthly and annual memberships are available for singles and couples. Monthly rates are $65 to $80 for residents and $75 to $90 for nonresidents. Annual memberships are $150 to $300 for residents, and $200 to $400 for nonresidents. Annual members may have guests play for $5.

AMENITIES

Riverview has a large clubhouse with a grand ballroom, exercise room with showers, crafts room, indoor shuffleboard, six billiard tables, a TV lounge, and a full-time recreation director. In addition to golf, outdoor facilities include a heated pool, a lap pool, tennis courts, and horseshoe pits. There is a large laundry room, a pro shop, showers, private mailboxes, and evening security.

REVIEWER'S NOTES

Riverview is one of the larger RV parks in the area and also one of the nicer ones. The clubhouse, golf course, and other recreational amenities make this facility a good choice for either short-term or long-term stays in this area. Advance reservations are advised during the high season (October through April).

SNOWBIRD RV RESORT

1600 Joy Lane

Bullhead City, AZ 86430

(602) 768-2141

INDEPENDENT LIVING FACILITY

An adult RV park. Warm winters and gambling casinos less than five miles away.

HOUSING TYPES AVAILABLE

RV spaces with full hookups for your RV.

NUMBER OF SITES/UNITS

123 spaces.

LOCATION

Bullhead City and Laughlin, Nevada are thriving due to the popularity of casinos, especially with retirees. Hospital and medical facilities as well as shopping and other consumer services are within a five-mile radius. Lakes Mohave and Mead are a short drive away and many winter visitors bring their boats. Summer temperatures are often the highest in the nation but October through April are more temperate.

REQUIREMENTS/RESTRICTIONS

Adults (over 21) only. Pets permitted.

FEES

Spaces rent for $75 weekly, $220 monthly. Utilities and use of the recreational facilities in the park are included in the rent. There is a nine-hole golf course that is free to those renting on a monthly basis. Otherwise there is a modest greens fee, which changes seasonally.

AMENITIES

In addition to the golf course there is a pool and Jacuzzi. The clubhouse hosts both scheduled and impromptu activities.

REVIEWER'S NOTES

Snowbird is attractive to golfers as well as gamblers. The park is well maintained and rents are moderate for the area. Transportation is not provided so your own car is necessary. Advance reservations are strongly recommended.

CHANDLER VILLAS

101 South Yucca Street

Chandler, AZ 85224

(602) 899-7650

Rent

Robin Holloway, Marketing Representative

INDEPENDENT LIVING FACILITY

A rental retirement community for mature adults desiring catered or assisted living services. Established in 1985 and owned and operated by Chandler Villas and Associates, a Chicago investment group.

HOUSING TYPES AVAILABLE

One- and two-bedroom apartments available in five models in 15 buildings (3 single story and 12 two story) on over eight acres. The smallest one-bedroom apartments have 450 sq ft; other one bedrooms range from 650 to 717 sq ft; two bedrooms from 830 to 900. Apartments are spacious with extra-large bathrooms. All apartments are wheelchair accessible and have walk-in showers, grab bars, and wide doors. Apartments have either balconies or patios. All open to the outside.

NUMBER OF SITES/UNITS

164 apartments.

LOCATION

Chandler Villas is located in Chandler, a community about 10 minutes south of Tempe and Mesa, Arizona. It is somewhat less congested in winter than those cities—something the Villas stress. Chandler is also growing as a city and offers a number of convenient services and amenities including shopping, recreation, physicians' offices, and churches. The local area hospital—Chandler Regional—is only a few blocks away, and Phoenix airport is about a 20-minute drive.

REQUIREMENTS/RESTRICTIONS

Age 55 and over preferred; pets are allowed.

FEES

One-bedroom unfurnished apartments rent from $555 to $735 per month per person; two bedrooms, from $865 to $935. There is an additional person charge of $50 per month. The monthly rent includes 24-hour staff and an emergency call system, bi-monthly housekeeping services, scheduled transportation, social activities, and the use of all community amenities (except dining). Meals are optional. Breakfast costs $65 per month per person; lunch, $125; and dinner, $75. Covered parking is $15 per month. Chandler Villas also caters to winter visitors, offering furnished one- or two-bedroom apartments that come with television, dishes and cooking equipment, and linens. One bedrooms are $1300 per month; two bedrooms, $1400. Since only a limited number are available it is advisable to plan ahead.

AMENITIES

Chandler Villas apartments all have 24-hour emergency call systems and the larger units have dishwashers and washer/dryer hookups. Community amenities include a swimming pool and Jacuzzi, an attractive community center and dining room including a private dining area, a beauty and barber shop, a convenience store, and scheduled transportation. Chandler Villas also offers more extensive personal care/assisted living services such as medication reminders, meal delivery, and assistance in bathing or dressing for an additional monthly fee.

REVIEWER'S NOTES

This is an unpretentious, pleasant rental community located in a residential area of Chandler. The area is less crowded than Mesa but still convenient to area services and amenities. The community itself offers a wide range of services mostly available on an optional basis, making it attractive to a wide range of retirees with different needs.

COTTONWOOD VILLAGE

201 East Mingus Avenue

Cottonwood, AZ 86326

(602) 634-2956

Rent   **Elaine Brenner, General Manager**

INDEPENDENT LIVING FACILITY

Cottonwood Village offers a catered lifestyle in secure surroundings for retirees in a small-town setting. Established in 1985 by Basic American Medical, Inc., it is now managed by Marriott.

HOUSING TYPES AVAILABLE

Three models are available: studio/alcove; one bedroom; and two bedroom, two bath. Approximate square footage in these models is 400, 550, and 700 sq ft. All apartments have kitchenettes that include microwave ovens. A single multi-story building houses the whole facility. All hallways are interior and there is elevator service on each floor. Emergency call boxes have been installed in all apartments.

NUMBER OF SITES/UNITS

66 apartments.

LOCATION

Cottonwood is located two hours (100 miles) north of Phoenix. Cottonwood Village is centrally located in this small town and is quite near a hospital with more than 90 beds, the public library, and the post office. Scheduled transportation is provided to supermarkets and shopping.

REQUIREMENTS/RESTRICTIONS

No specified minimum age but current residents average about 70 years old. Pets are permitted.

FEES

Monthly rent averages between $750 (studio) and $1100 (two bedroom) and includes two meals daily, utilities, housekeeping, and maintenance. Additional services such as assistance with bathing, medication reminders, grocery shopping, and escort service are available at a small extra charge.

AMENITIES

Scheduled activities such as exercise classes or crafts classes are offered to residents. Trips to cultural events and local points of interest are scheduled frequently. Residents also participate in special interest clubs, evening discussions, bible studies, and film nights. The common rooms and dining area are attractively furnished. The staff is also available to help with questions on medical and insurance bills.

REVIEWER'S NOTES

Although Cottonwood Village is somewhat smaller than other facilities listed in this book, we felt it should be included. Its location puts it far away from congested areas and could be suitable for persons desiring to live in a small town. We found this facility to have an exceptionally friendly and caring staff. This area offers a mild four-season climate that has attracted many long-time Phoenix residents. There are quite a few retirees here that have relocated from within the state. If you want to visit this area, it makes a very pleasant day trip from Phoenix.

COLTER VILLAGE

Rent

5125 North 58th Avenue

Glendale, AZ 85301

(602) 931-5800

INDEPENDENT LIVING FACILITY

A retirement apartment community with meals included. Assisted independent living apartments are also available; there is a skilled nursing facility on site. Established in 1984 by Basic American Retirement Community and now owned by Western Health Care of Boise, Idaho.

HOUSING TYPES AVAILABLE

Small individual apartments: studio, enlarged studio, and one bedroom (all with very small kitchenettes). The largest model available is under 500 sq ft. The apartments are nice but not fancy. They would serve well for a person living alone or couples not requiring a lot of space. Some of the apartments have been designated for people needing assistance with personal care or those having physical limitations. Additionally, there is a skilled nursing center within the community. All apartments are off enclosed hallways and the complex is on two levels with elevators. There is a 24-hour emergency call system in all apartments.

NUMBER OF SITES/UNITS

206 apartments.

LOCATION

Colter Village is located in Glendale, which borders on Phoenix. This area is convenient to services and public transportation and is 20 minutes from downtown Phoenix. Colter Village provides resident transportation for shopping and medical needs, so a car is not a necessity. The area immediately surrounding the facility is mixed moderate income residential and commercial businesses.

REQUIREMENTS/RESTRICTIONS

Minimum age 55. Small pets are allowed.

FEES

Studio apartments rent for $750 monthly, enlarged studios for $1200, and one bedrooms for $1300. This fee covers two restaurant-style meals daily and all utilities including telephone. Additional charges are assessed for the assisted living apartments depending on the services required. Skilled nursing charges are currently $82.50 (private) and $65 (semi-private) daily.

AMENITIES

The recreation and common area contains games and crafts rooms, a TV lounge, library, gift shop, laundry rooms, and a restaurant-style dining room. Social activities are scheduled frequently. There is secured storage available to residents. There is a Jacuzzi but no pool. The scheduled transportation is a plus for those not wanting to drive or own a car.

REVIEWER'S NOTES

Colter Village offers a secure environment for those not wanting the responsibility of home maintenance or the responsibility of meal preparation. The apartments allow you to maintain your independence while providing the security and reassurance of nearby health care services. Apartments are basic and functional in design and not elaborate. This could be a good choice for people uncomfortable in fancy settings but desirous of quality services.

GLENCROFT

Buy

8611 North 67th Avenue

Glendale, AZ 85302

(602) 939-9475

GLENCROFT-NORTH

Buy

20802 North Cave Creek

Phoenix, AZ 85024

(602) 569-0508

INDEPENDENT LIVING FACILITY

A Christian retirement community that welcomes all faiths. Established in 1973 by the Friendship Retirement Corporation, a corporation founded by the Mennonite, Apostolic Christian, and Friends Churches in the Phoenix area.

HOUSING TYPES AVAILABLE

Glencroft garden apartments (240), arranged around eight courts of 30 units, and 96 condominiums. Apartments are available for purchase in three floor plans: one bedroom, one bath; two bedrooms, one bath; and two bedrooms, two baths. The square footage ranges from approximately 600 to almost 900 depending on the floor plan. In addition, 120 villa apartments—small one-bedroom or studio (efficiency) units—are available for rent. Glencroft Towers provides subsidized housing in 102 apartments with three different floor plans ranging from studios to two bedrooms, one bath. The care center provides three levels of supervised licensed care including skilled nursing care. Only the garden apartments are ground level. All other apartments are contained in multi-level, elevator equipped buildings.

Glencroft-North garden apartments are available in five floor plans ranging from one bedroom with one bath, with a little over 700 sq ft, to the deluxe two bedroom, two bath, with 1068 sq ft. The other three floor plans have two bedrooms and one bath, with square footage between 787 and 894. (The square footage is approximate.) Each unit is single story with a white stucco Spanish facade and an attached covered carport. These newly built apartments are equipped with range, refrigerator, dishwasher, and washer/dryer hookups. The entire community is enclosed by a white stucco wall for privacy and security.

NUMBER OF SITES/UNITS

Glencroft: over 1000 residents.

Glencroft-North: still in development, it is on 20 acres. About one-quarter of the garden apartments are completed.

LOCATION

Glencroft occupies 36 acres in Glendale adjacent to north Phoenix. This particular area is near shopping, hospitals and doctors, golf courses, and other businesses. The immediate area is mostly residential. The Phoenix airport is about 25 minutes away.

REQUIREMENTS/RESTRICTIONS

No specific age requirement for nonsubsidized housing. Government subsidized apartments require that the occupant(s) be at least 62 years old or disabled and meet minimum financial standards on income and assets. Pets are permitted only in the subsidized apartments. All renters are required to take at least one meal daily in the community dining room (for an additional charge).

FEES

Glencroft garden apartments and condominium apartments are purchased but not deeded to the owner. It is equivalent to an endowment, with the apartment ownership reverting to Glencroft when the resident passes away or decides to leave. This is an example of how the system works: You might pay $50,000 when you purchase the apartment at age 60. When you leave the apartment (regardless of length of occupancy), you or your estate will receive 45 percent of your $50,000 equity with no interest. Glencroft keeps the remaining 55 percent. If the purchase is made when you are 70, your equity is 55 percent and Glencroft retains 45 percent upon death or departure. The percentage of your equity varies from 45 to 75 percent, depending on your age or that of the younger spouse at the time of purchase. Glencroft uses its portion for upkeep on the facility and for causes as it sees fit. The purchase price (endowment) for garden apartments and condominiums begins at under $40,000 and goes up to just over $50,000, depending on the size. A monthly service charge is assessed for each unit, from $108 to $167, again depending on unit size. Residents of apartments with two occupants pay an additional $8 monthly. The service charge covers grounds care, building maintenance, water, trash collection, sewer, appliance repair, and scheduled local transportation. Apartment rental rates (nonsubsidized) are $335 (studio) and $398 (one bedroom) and include utilities, facility use, and local transportation. All residents who are renting must purchase at least one meal daily in the restaurant-style community dining room at a cost of $110 monthly. Government-subsidized (section 8) apartments rent for various prices depending on your income and assets. You need to provide financial documentation to determine your eligibility and your monthly rent rate. One meal daily must be purchased for an additional fee. There is about a two-year wait for these apartments. Care center rates vary with the level of care and services required. Charges are assessed separately from the purchase price or rental payments.

Glencroft-North current pricing ranges from $42,000 to $62,700 depending on the floor plan. These prices are lower than average because of the endowment, not because they are inferior in any discernible way. Monthly service charges range between $143 and $176 for single occupancy, plus $7 for a second person. This charge covers grounds care, sewer, water, trash removal, building maintenance, and appliance repair. It also includes recreation facilities. Fees on proposed assisted living facilities not yet available. See Glencroft fee section for equity formulas.

AMENITIES

Glencroft recreational activities are coordinated by a full-time director of activities. Facilities include an indoor pool, activity rooms, billiards, shuffleboard, a small library, and an auditorium/chapel with nondenominational worship services. Transportation to shopping is provided, so a car is nice but not necessary. Organized trips and outings are planned at additional cost. Maid service is available for a modest fee.

Glencroft-North recreational facilities include an indoor pool and spa (under construction), game rooms, a putting green, and a woodworking shop. Twenty-four-hour security will be provided at the entrance. Medical facilities, shopping, banks, parks, and golf courses are 10 minutes away. The community offers a Christian, caring environment with pastoral care and chaplaincy programs. Transportation to shopping and medical facilities is provided by the facility.

REVIEWER'S NOTES

Glencroft offers a wide range of services in a Christian and caring environment at affordable prices; it can be viewed as a lifecare community in philosophy. You have a variety of housing choices depending on your needs and income level. The "independent living" housing has attractive landscaping and a warm, private feeling through the court design. There is a strong Christian focus but it is not necessary to hold those beliefs to be a resident. This community has a lot for those who appreciate the values and community spirit that is fostered here. The financial complexities of the endowment concept may be confusing or discouraging, but Glencroft has nearly 100 percent occupancy rate and maintains waiting lists for many units. It appears to be worthy of further investigation if this kind of lifestyle appeals to you.

Glencroft-North, although not yet completed, promises to be as successful as its sister community, Glencroft in Glendale. A visit should be made to both facilities in order to get an idea of the potential lifestyle. Glencroft-North should have units available, while Glencroft always remains at near capacity.

GREENFIELDS

Rent

13617 North 55th Avenue

Glendale, AZ 85304

(602) 938-5500

INDEPENDENT LIVING FACILITY

Greenfields offers independent living apartments as well as supervisory care for both short- and long-term residents. Built in 1985 by FMH Foundation. The new owner (as of June 1989) is Danaco.

HOUSING TYPES AVAILABLE

Apartments are contained in a three-story building arranged around a center courtyard. The hallways are interior and there are elevators in each wing. Studio apartments are approximately 400 sq ft in size and have kitchenettes. One-bedroom apartments range from about 550 to 600 sq ft and the two-bedroom units (all with one bath) are approximately 700 sq ft. Some models have balconies or patios. Supervisory care is provided in either private or semiprivate rooms.

NUMBER OF SITES/UNITS

146 apartments (independent); 92 supervisory care beds.

LOCATION

Greenfields' Glendale location provides for easy access to both Sun City and North Phoenix services and attractions. Thunderbird Samaritan Hospital is directly across the street from the facility, and banks and supermarkets are nearby as well. Transportation to doctors and shopping is provided by Greenfields within a seven-mile radius.

REQUIREMENTS/RESTRICTIONS

Adults only (no specific minimum age). Pets under 15 pounds welcome.

FEES

Studio apartments rent from $760 per month; one bedroom, $1050; and two bedroom, $1435. This monthly charge includes two meals daily and all utilities except telephones. Additional services covered include maid service, transportation, free laundry rooms, and three activity directors. Supervisory-care rooms range from $600 to $1200 monthly and include three meals daily in addition to 24-hour staff supervision. If space permits, short-term occupancy is available for a charge of $40 daily.

AMENITIES

Apartments have emergency call systems that are monitored around the clock. Bathrooms have safety bars, sit-down showers, and wide doors that open outward for easy accessibility. Recreational activities include a pool and spa, arts and crafts room, exercise class, shuffleboard, TV lounge, and library. Special activities are scheduled almost daily and frequently include ice cream socials, bingo, movies, dances, monthly collective birthday parties, and outings and trips. Meals are served restaurant style and vary daily. Steaks, chops, and fish are mainstays at dinner, and there is always a salad bar. Wine and beer are also available.

REVIEWER'S NOTES

Although Greenfields is under new management, the new owner was on site the day we stopped by. The staff was friendly and knowledgeable. Common areas were nicely furnished and the grounds well kept. Seasonal visitors are welcome when space is available and adult day care is offered for area residents (or visiting parents) needing some supervision combined with social interaction. This facility really seems to accommodate all age groups. Active seniors need not feel that this community is only for more frail individuals. There appeared to be good integration of all residents, as well as a variety of special activities suiting more specialized interests. Average age of the residents is between 65 and 70 years.

THUNDERBIRD GARDENS

Rent

5401 West Dailey Street

Glendale, AZ 85306

(602) 938-0414

INDEPENDENT LIVING FACILITY

A large apartment complex in a convenient location. Major medical facilities within walking distance. Established in 1987 as a for-profit venture. Currently operated by American Opportunity Foundation with a not-for-profit status.

HOUSING TYPES AVAILABLE

Five floor plans are available: studio; one bedroom, one bath; one bedroom, two bath; two bedroom, one bath; and two bedroom, two bath. Approximate square footage ranges from 420 to 1140. The building is multi-winged, with three enclosed floors (no outdoor hallways). The facility is rectangular in shape with three private center courtyards. The courtyards are landscaped and have ponds in addition to the pool and shuffleboard. The community dining room looks out on the courtyards. The apartments are of average size with good closet space (most have a large walk-in closet) and fair storage space.

NUMBER OF SITES/UNITS

348 units.

LOCATION

Thunderbird Gardens' Glendale address provides easy access to both Sun City and Phoenix. Thunderbird Hospital is just across the street and many physicians have offices in the immediate area. Scheduled transportation is provided, and all services, retail stores, and major religious denominations are within a five-mile radius. A car is not a necessity, but would offer convenience. Travel time to the airport and downtown Phoenix averages around 30 minutes.

REQUIREMENTS/RESTRICTIONS

Minimum age 62. Small pets are welcome.

FEES

Studio apartments rent for $585 per month; one bedrooms, $790 and $1050; and two bedroom models, $1050 and $1520. Services included in the rent include: one meal daily, weekly housekeeping, security, the use of recreation and common areas, and scheduled transportation. Seasonal and short-term leases may be slightly higher and are contingent upon availability. Check with a leasing agent about rates and furnished apartments. This is a modified HUD-subsidized facility—although most residents do not qualify—so again ask the agent for guidelines.

AMENITIES

There are several very thoughtful amenities that pertain to resident security. In addition to the emergency call boxes in each apartment there is a resident check system every evening and morning. This is accomplished by security and personnel checking each door for a colored tag on the door knob. If the tag is not out, a staff member will first try to reach the resident by phone and so forth until the resident is accounted for. Recreational and social activities are scheduled frequently. Amenities include a pool, lounges, a card room, and shuffleboard courts.

REVIEWER'S NOTES

Thunderbird Gardens offers many amenities at a moderate price (for the area). We found the interiors of this community to be quite pleasant, with an elegant but comfortable dining room and common rooms. The hallways are carpeted and extra wide. We cannot account for the high number of vacancies (more than 25 percent) except for its very large size. Based on those we met, the staff members are quite friendly and knowledgeable. The security systems in place are quite good and seem to be among the best, all around, that we have seen.

GREEN VALLEY

Green Valley, AZ 85622

(800) 528-4930; (602) 625-4441;

(602) 648-0800 (for resales)

Buy

INDEPENDENT LIVING FACILITY

A planned retirement community established in 1972. Approximately 80 percent of the homes were developed by Fairfield Green Valley, Inc.

HOUSING TYPES AVAILABLE

Homes and townhomes (duplexes) with 14 different models; mostly two-bedroom units with some three bedroom/den. Square footage ranges from 1060 to 2508, depending on the model. The homes are single level with a unique southwestern territorial design: a distinctive red brick (adobe bricks) look to them and in most cases a flat-roof-type design (the roof is not actually flat but appears to be). The developer has a program that allows for home customization.

NUMBER OF SITES/UNITS

Over 17,000 people now live in Green Valley in over 7000 homes. New models as well as resales are available.

LOCATION

Green Valley is located 27 miles south of Tucson just off I-19 in a wide valley in the foothills of the Santa Rita Mountains. The scenery is beautiful and the setting attractive. The location gives you rapid access to Tucson and the airport.

REQUIREMENTS/RESTRICTIONS

One resident in each household must be at least 55.

FEES

New homes start at $81,000 and climb to $185,400, depending on the model. Residents pay homeowners' association fees for maintenance of streets and common lands. These fees range from $336 to $420 per year per household depending on where your home is located. Residents also pay $189 per year per household for membership in Green Valley Recreation Association, which entitles you to use all the recreational facilities except the golf course.

AMENITIES

Green Valley has every recreational amenity you can imagine from swimming, golf courses, and tennis to crafts and hobbies, classes, and clubs. Daily golf fees run from $15 to $26, depending on the season. The community offers all types of amenities from shopping to churches. Doctors' offices are local. However, the nearest hospitals are in Tucson. We were told, however, that there is an excellent paramedic service.

REVIEWER'S NOTES

One of the oldest retirement communities in Arizona, Green Valley is well established with active organizations and clubs. It has a small-town atmosphere and is not congested. There is very little crime and people stress the security and safety aspects of living here. A recent survey showed the median age of residents to be 70 years. The homes are comfortable and provide a cozy feeling.

KINGMAN RANCH

1201 Jagerson Avenue

Kingman, AZ 86401

(602) 757-2127

INDEPENDENT LIVING FACILITY

A master-planned mobile and manufactured home community in Kingman, which is about 45 minutes east of the Bullhead City/Laughlin area. Established in 1987.

HOUSING TYPES AVAILABLE

Mobile and manufactured homes in a variety of sizes and designs are available for purchase on site. Each home has a large covered patio, carport, landscaping, central air conditioning, and a separate storage building.

NUMBER OF SITES/UNITS

406 mobile home spaces on 80 acres.

LOCATION

Kingman is located in northwest Arizona on Interstate 40. Phoenix is a three-and-one-half-hour drive and Las Vegas can be reached in less than two hours. Although Kingman is still under 20,000 in population, it lies within Mohave County, which is reported to be the fastest-growing county in the country. Kingman has an 83-bed hospital and there are a number of physicians in the area, banks, supermarkets, and mini-malls. A small airport has daily flights to and from Phoenix, Las Vegas, and Bullhead City on Golden Pacific Airlines. For those who enjoy fishing, boating, and other outdoor recreational activities Kingman is conveniently located. Lakes Mohave, Mead, and Havasu are all within a 90-minute drive. Hualapai Mountain Park, just 14 miles away, offers 15 miles of hiking trails in a ponderosa pine forest. The city is at an elevation of 3330 feet. Year-round temperatures are milder in the summer and cooler in the winter than Phoenix or Las Vegas. The terrain is high desert with sparse vegetation. Lack of industry makes Kingman's air healthy for people with breathing problems.

REQUIREMENTS/RESTRICTIONS

No specific age requirement. All adult park at present. Pets are allowed.

FEES

Home prices begin in the low $40,000 range. Larger and customized models will run more. All home prices include the covered porch, air-conditioning, storage shed, and desert landscaping. Monthly space rental of $175 includes water, sewer, garbage pickup, and cable TV hookup.

AMENITIES

A community recreation area provides residents with a pool, spa, lounge, and billiard room. Utilities are housed underground to maintain a natural park-like setting. The Mohave County sheriff's department is adjacent to the facility and its presence adds security.

REVIEWER'S NOTES

The Kingman area is attracting new residents at a higher rate than other Arizona cities. Kingman Ranch provides affordable housing in a pleasant setting. We felt the area to be somewhat remote but with adequate services for residents. Many retirees appreciate the small-town atmosphere and the accessibility of recreational facilities. The climate, which is warm and dry with more distinctive seasonal changes, is another plus.

APACHE WELLS

2215 North 56th Street

Mesa, AZ 85205

(602) 832-1331

Buy
Emily Bartee; Joanne Johnson, Agents

INDEPENDENT LIVING FACILITY

A planned community on 600 acres featuring a championship 18-hole golf course. Established in 1970. Individual home owners now own the development.

HOUSING TYPES AVAILABLE

Custom-built single-family homes make up about 10 percent of the residences. The remaining 90 percent are manufactured—prefabricated mobile homes trucked in to your lot—but these are very attractive and do not resemble trailer-park models. All the existing homes are attractively landscaped in the Southwest desert style. As you can choose your own home, no set square footage exists. Most of the homes for resale range from about 1100 to 2100 sq ft.

NUMBER OF SITES/UNITS

2250, with some undeveloped lots still available.

LOCATION

Apache Wells is located in northeast Mesa, still relatively uncrowded. Some of the orange groves are still standing. The Superstition Mountains are clearly visible to the east, and the McDowell Mountains and Four Peaks are visible to the north. Hospitals, doctors' offices, shopping, and entertainment are a short 10-minute drive. Your own car is the recommended means of transportation, as there is no public bus nearby. Dial-a-Ride taxi is available. Banking, restaurant, cocktail lounge, convenience market, and community church are all within Apache Wells itself. The freeway to Phoenix and its airport is 15 minutes to the south, and once on the freeway it is less than an hour to most destinations in Phoenix. Those who enjoy fishing and boating will find three human-made reservoirs less than an hour away.

REQUIREMENTS/RESTRICTIONS

One resident in each household must be at least 55. Children are welcome as guests.

FEES

Resale homes are on the market from $35,000 to $100,000. Lots for new homes start at $25,000 and climb to $40,000 for a lot adjacent to the golf course. Homeowner fee is $13.75 per month. This is obligatory and does not include golf but does give you clubhouse and pool privileges. Membership fees for the golf course run from $8000 to $10,000 one-time fee in addition to greens fee.

AMENITIES

The championship golf course, which is the focal point of this community, includes its own pro shop and resident pros. Only members paying the golf membership are allowed to play, but you may play as a guest of a member. The recreation hall is well equipped, large, and attractive (it is open to all residents). Facilities consist of an olympic-size heated pool and spa, arts and crafts hobby center, tennis courts, putting green, exercise studio, dining rooms, and cocktail lounges. There is also an abundance of planned and unplanned activities and events. Security is organized by neighborhood patrol.

REVIEWER'S NOTES

Apache Wells is an established and attractive golf-oriented community. Residents tend to be very active and many are still employed. Resale homes represent the best value and allow for someone to have a home and golf membership for around $80,000. The manufactured homes should be considered as they are well constructed and difficult to tell from conventional homes. The size of the development (600 acres) and number of residents make this community spacious and not overcrowded. The surrounding area contributes a rural feeling. More than 75 percent of the residents remain year round.

DREAMLAND VILLA

6000 East University Drive

Mesa, AZ 85205

(602) 832-6202

Buy   **Farnsworth Realty**

INDEPENDENT LIVING FACILITY

A planned retirement community; one of Arizona's first. Developed by Farnsworth Construction, circa 1960. Resale homes only.

HOUSING TYPES AVAILABLE

Single-family homes of block construction. Homes built in Dreamland Villa are all single story, ranch style. Most homes have two bedrooms, although there are a few with three. Square footage is anywhere between 800 and 2300 sq ft, depending on the model. All the homes have desert/gravel front yards (very well kept) and about half have grass lawns in the back. There were about 50 homes for sale at the time of our visit. This number is proportionately small compared to other nonretirement areas in Mesa, a good sign of a stable facility.

NUMBER OF SITES/UNITS

4125 residents. No new building sites available.

LOCATION

East Mesa, which is becoming quite developed, is the site of Dreamland Villa. The Velda Rose Estates, a smaller retirement development, borders to the north and is virtually indistinguishable from this development. All the necessary conveniences are within a 15-minute drive. The freeway to Phoenix and the airport is only 10 minutes to the south. The city bus is at least a 10-minute walk. Service is sporadic and the bus line is not much used. As with the rest of Mesa, Dial-a-Ride serves Dreamland Villa. Most major religious denominations have services a short drive away.

REQUIREMENTS/RESTRICTIONS

Minimum age is 55 for at least one member of the household. Children are welcome as guests.

FEES

Homes for sale at the time of this writing were priced from $49,000 to $100,000. Homes for lease are sometimes available. Farnsworth Realty may be contacted for further information on both types of listings. Other real estate companies (Century 21, Coldwell Banker, and so on) had a few homes listed as well. Homeowners' fees are modest—$37.50 per person per year.

AMENITIES

Facilities include one nine-hole golf course with a moderate greens fee that varies with the season, and two clubhouses/recreation centers at either end of the development. Both centers have pools, an arts and crafts room, and social rooms. The community has its own library and restaurant. There are dances and bingo as the weather gets cooler. All common areas are at ground level with fair to good disabled accessibility.

REVIEWER'S NOTES

Dreamland Villa has aged very well over its 30-year history. Visits made in the early 1960s reveal how little has changed since then. The homes and yards are still immaculately kept and the clubhouses have been almost as well maintained. The streets are wide and the blocks are long with very little traffic except for evening walkers. The community is quiet and somewhat less "activity oriented" than some of the others visited. It appears to be very solid and affordable to those wishing to buy a home in a quiet, clean community.

GOOD LIFE RV RESORT

3403 East Main Street

Mesa, AZ 85213

(602) 832-4990; (800) 999-4990

INDEPENDENT LIVING FACILITY

An adults-only RV park in the heart of Mesa's RV "paradise." In operation for over 10 years.

HOUSING TYPES AVAILABLE

Recreational vehicles only. There may be units offered for rent in the park, but in most cases you must bring your own RV. All spaces have full hookups.

NUMBER OF SITES/UNITS

Over 1200 individual spaces located on 58 acres.

LOCATION

Good Life is yet another RV resort on East Main Street in Mesa. It is conveniently located, within a five-mile radius of major hospitals, physicians' clinics, shopping, churches, golf courses, banking, and restaurants. Superstition Freeway provides easy access to Phoenix and the west valley.

REQUIREMENTS/RESTRICTIONS

Adults only. Pets are allowed only in the special pet section of the facility.

FEES

The daily rate is $19; weekly, $110. Both include electricity, sewer, water, and refuse collection. The monthly rate of $310 does not include electricity. The 12-month annual rate for a regular space is $1575, with premium spaces (location and larger size) ranging from $1650 to $1660. Annual rates do not include electricity. Recreational facilities and participation in scheduled activities are available to all residents. The annual rate may allow you to leave your RV at Good Life when you return home in the summer.

AMENITIES

The 27,000-sq-ft activity center is located in the center of the facility. It provides residents with rooms for arts and crafts, cards and games, billiards, educational classes, TV, a library, physical fitness activities, special interest club meetings, and special dinners. There is a large dance floor with regularly scheduled dances (square and round, ballroom, folk). Nondenominational church services as well as bible study groups are held weekly. Two swimming and therapy pools and 24 lighted shuffleboard courts are also available for residents' use. Laundry rooms and shower rooms are placed around the park. The special pet walking area, located on the outer corner of the facility, should keep both pet owners and nonowners happy.

REVIEWER'S NOTES

Good Life RV Resort appeared to be a very nice facility, especially for couples or individuals seeking a place with many activity options. The size and layout of this facility make it possible to avoid the crowd by requesting a space on the periphery of the complex. Still, the majority of residents seem to have chosen this particular park because of the number of activities and the companionship of other residents. We found Good Life to be clean and well managed.

GREENFIELD VILLAGE RV RESORT

111 South Greenfield Road

Mesa, AZ 85206

(602) 832-6400; (800) 832-3220

INDEPENDENT LIVING FACILITY

An adults-only RV resort in the heart of Mesa's RV "paradise." Operated by Premier RV Resorts of Arizona.

HOUSING TYPES AVAILABLE

Self-contained RV units or trailers. A lease plan is available for some units.

NUMBER OF SITES/UNITS

Approximately 800 spaces located on 60 acres.

LOCATION

Greenfield Village is located just off of East Main Street in Mesa, in the area with the densest population of retirees. This area is both popular and desirable because of the abundance of businesses that cater to the needs of retirees. Almost all services (both necessary and convenient) are located within a five-mile radius. Traffic is quite heavy during the winter months.

REQUIREMENTS/RESTRICTIONS

Adults only. Small pets allowed but must be contained at all times.

FEES

All spaces have full hookups and concrete pad. Daily, weekly, and monthly rates are seasonal. High season (December-March) rates are $25 per day, $140 per week, and $400 per month. Low season (April-November) rates are $16 per day, $95 per week, and $240 per month. The annual rate is $2100. Daily and weekly rates include electricity. All spaces include water, sewer, cable TV, telephone hookups, and the use of recreational facilities.

Spaces may be offered for purchase. To find out more about this, contact the facility. The price range should be in the $10,000 to $20,000 range.

AMENITIES

Greenfield Village features a six-and-one-half-acre recreation area with an olympic-size pool, tennis courts, a recreation hall with a dance floor, laundry and shower facilities, arts and crafts rooms, TV lounges, an exercise room, and barbecue areas. Celebrity entertainment, dances, and bingo occur throughout the season. The entrance to the park has a 24-hour manned guard station. We have reviewed this facility as a rental community. As we mentioned, spaces may be available for purchase.

REVIEWER'S NOTES

Greenfield Village offers a somewhat more elaborate setting to its residents. The recreation area buildings are designed in the Spanish style with tile roofs and outdoor fountains. Rates are a little higher than average during the high season and the residents and vehicles tend to reflect that. There is a less transitory feeling at Greenfield Village than at some of the neighboring parks. Premier RV Resorts operates similar resorts in the Phoenix area: Golden Vista, 3710 South Goldfield Road, Apache Junction, AZ 85219; Roadhaven, 1000 South Idaho Road, Apache Junction, AZ 85219; and Paradise, 10950 West Union Hills Drive, Sun City, AZ 85373. Information also can be obtained by calling this central toll-free number: (800) 832-3220.

LEISURE WORLD

908 South Power Road

Mesa, AZ 85206

(602) 832-3232

Buy

INDEPENDENT LIVING FACILITY

A planned community in a country-club-style setting. Established in 1972 by Rossmoor Development, currently a division of Western Savings and Loan.

HOUSING TYPES AVAILABLE

Single-family homes with square footage ranging from 996 sq ft to over 2000 sq ft. Duplexes begin at 851 sq ft in a one bedroom, one bath and exceed 1300 sq ft in the large two-bedroom, two-bath floor plans. Condominium square footage is 1300 sq ft. New homesites are available with your choice of floor plan. There are also pre-owned homes for sale.

NUMBER OF SITES/UNITS

2270 units presently, with 300 currently available for sale. New homesites are expected to be available until 1995.

LOCATION

Leisure World is located in the more recently developed southeastern part of Mesa. Necessary services and shopping are close by, and a newly built hospital is right next door. This part of Mesa has many retirement communities/facilities, but Leisure World is the largest and most established. The freeway that serves the Phoenix metropolitan area is convenient, so travel time to the airport and downtown Phoenix is about one-half hour.

REQUIREMENTS/RESTRICTIONS

Minimum age 55 (for couples); spouses over 45 are welcome. Children or grandchildren under 18 may visit. Pets are permitted, but leash laws are enforced.

FEES

Condominiums are available from $79,600, duplexes from $81,100, and single-family homes from $77,450. Duplexes and single-family homes include initial landscaping and lot. Special options are available. Single-family custom homes can cost up to $200,000. The standard service fee for duplexes and homes is $86 per month.

AMENITIES

Two private golf courses and driving range are available (additional annual charge, $846 for all courses; $540 for Lake course only). Daily rates are also available. The multi-million dollar recreation centers are open to all residents and offer a vast array of activities. Twenty-four-hour security begins at the entrance. Clubs abound at Leisure World, with groups devoted to almost anything imaginable. The recreation centers are beautifully designed and landscaped, one with a small lake and a clock tower.

REVIEWER'S NOTES

Leisure World is an attractive planned community for those who are looking for an active and sophisticated retirement site. The recreation centers are enormous and the hub of most activity. There are more moderately priced developments in the area but they don't offer the range of activities or the country-club look and feel that Leisure World offers.

MESA REGAL RV RESORT

4700 East Main
Street
Mesa, AZ 85205
(602) 830-2821

INDEPENDENT LIVING FACILITY

Mesa Regal is an adult RV park for short-term visitors and year-round residents. Family-owned and operated for more than 10 years.

HOUSING TYPES AVAILABLE

RV and park model trailers are permitted. Leasing or subletting of RVs and trailers is not permitted. Annual residents may add awnings, storage rooms, or Arizona rooms, but City of Mesa permits are required.

NUMBER OF SITES/UNITS

1860 spaces located on over 110 acres.

LOCATION

Mesa Regal is in East Mesa. The area is populated with similar facilities and apartments for retirees. This RV park boasts that it is within a two-block radius of eight restaurants, eight doctors, a supermarket, four banks, six clothing stores, and other small specialty shops. True, but they are long blocks. This is quite beneficial, since coping with winter time traffic and parking can be a nightmarish experience. Summer does provide full-time residents with blessedly plentiful parking and only moderately congested city streets.

Judging from the fact that this area remains extremely popular with yearly winter visitors, the benefits appear to outweigh the negative points.

REQUIREMENTS/RESTRICTIONS

An adults-only park. Pet owners must be in designated pet section. No smoking is permitted in common areas. Mesa Regal has a long list of restrictions designed for the benefit of all residents. It is advisable to request a copy of this detailed information from the facility.

FEES

Daily rates are $15; weekly rates are $85 including electricity. Monthly rates are $198 not including electricity. The annual rate, which is based on space size, ranges from $1300 to $1420 not including electricity. Mesa Regal was offering special incentive annual rates at the time of our visit and may still be. Be sure to inquire about this if you contact them.

AMENITIES

A wide array of activities, both social and recreational, exist at Mesa Regal. There are three heated pools and a very large Jacuzzi, and 11 pool tables. An 800-seat amphitheater wraps around lighted tennis courts, 24 shuffle board courts, and a volleyball court. The activity complex contains classrooms, arts and crafts rooms, workshops, a beauty salon, and an in-park travel agency. Two ballrooms with full kitchen host special potluck and buffet dinners as well as dances. There are also several laundry facilities around the park.

REVIEWER'S NOTES

Mesa Regal was one of the largest facilities of this type we visited. Its proximity to outside services, coupled with the many conveniences on site, makes it an almost autonomous community. The many rules and regulations enforced by the park may be intimidating to some, but the regimentation does serve to keep everything running like clockwork. If you are tired of the come-as-you-are RV parks, Mesa Regal may be ideal for you. On the other hand, if you like a place with more relaxed standards, this park might be too structured. All else aside, Mesa Regal is a fine example of a clean, well-run RV park.

THE ORCHARD

108 North Greenfield Road

Mesa, AZ 85205

(602) 832-7334

Rent

INDEPENDENT LIVING FACILITY

Retirement apartments for healthy seniors who are already Arizona residents. Established in 1984.

HOUSING TYPES AVAILABLE

All apartments have the same one-bedroom, one-bath floor plan. Each unit has approximately 550 sq ft. First- or second-story apartments are available. There are no elevators and stairs and hallways are all exterior. Kitchens are small but there is a dining alcove. Bedrooms have walk-in closets.

NUMBER OF SITES/UNITS

700 units housed in 52 separate buildings.

LOCATION

The Orchard is located in east central Mesa. Medical facilities and hospitals are inside a five-mile radius. Shopping and banking services are a three-block walk away. The area is quite developed, with corner shopping centers, motels, RV and trailer parks, and small businesses. The winter months are known to bring heavy traffic to the area. However, if you do not mind a short walk there is no need to use your car for everyday necessities.

REQUIREMENTS/RESTRICTIONS

Arizona residency is required and the minimum age is 55. No pets are permitted. Minimum lease is for one year.

FEES

Monthly rent ranges from $229 to $309 and includes water and trash collection. All units are identical and price differences relate to location within the complex.

AMENITIES

The 9700-sq-ft Senior Citizen Center contains various arts and crafts rooms, a TV lounge, and a library. There are picnic areas and a heated pool in the grassy courtyard. Convenient laundry areas are located throughout the complex. There are on-site motel rooms for visitors. A chauffeured van is available to residents Monday through Friday for the small charge of 50 cents. The van travels around Mesa to popular destinations for shopping, medical needs, and entertainment.

REVIEWER'S NOTES

The Orchard offers inexpensive retirement community housing to Arizona residents. The complex is nicely landscaped and the apartments are modern and pleasant. There are many scheduled activities and events for residents, and the staff appears to be friendly and competent. While the area is congested, it is also convenient and many of the stores and businesses cater to retirees. All in all it is a good value for the money.

PALM GARDENS MOBILE HOME MANOR

2929 East Main Street

Mesa, AZ 85213

(602) 832-0290

HOUSING TYPES AVAILABLE

A mobile home and RV park. Mobile homes are in one area of this 50-acre park and RVs and travel trailers are in another. This facility caters to both long-term residents and winter visitors.

NUMBER OF SITES/UNITS

324 Mobile home spaces and 115 RV spaces.

LOCATION

Palm Gardens is in east central Mesa, which is within five miles of almost all Mesa has to offer. There are a number of mobile home communities concentrated in this area, and winter months bring heavy traffic. Local businesses and restaurants may offer discounts to retirees, and many parking lots are always full. The bright side to the congestion is that you may never want for company!

REQUIREMENTS/RESTRICTIONS

Minimum age is 55. No pets.

FEES

Mobile home spaces rent from $223 to $245 per month including water and sewer. Travel trailer and RV spaces run $16 daily, $95 weekly, $275 monthly, and $1395 yearly. Daily and weekly rates include electricity in addition to water and sewer. Mail is delivered to your space and telephone service is available. Resale mobile homes are sometimes available and can range from $10,000 to $30,000.

AMENITIES

There are two recreation facilities, both with heated pools, card and crafts rooms, and scheduled social activities. There are several laundry rooms located around the facility. Rental rates include use of all facilities.

REVIEWER'S NOTES

Its central location and well-kept grounds make this park attractive to winter visitors. Permanent residents will have the same benefits but must endure a long hot summer. The moderate annual fee of $1395 for RV owners makes it possible to avoid seasonal moving of your trailer or motor home.

ROYAL PALMS RETIREMENT

Rent

1825 North Stapley Drive

Mesa, AZ 85203

(602) 827-0407

INDEPENDENT LIVING FACILITY

A planned rental complex for older adults desiring independence with structure and security. Property built in 1985 and managed by Paul Ash Investment, Tucson.

HOUSING TYPES AVAILABLE

Studio to three-bedroom apartments. The studio, 480 sq ft; one bedroom, 665 to 780 sq ft; two bedroom, one bath, 885 sq ft; two bedroom, two bath, 1008 sq ft; and the three bedroom, two bath, 1296 sq ft. Apartments in this complex are very light and even the smaller units have a spacious feel. All are on a single floor, although there are two stories to the complex. The washer/dryer units are in the bathrooms, but the room is large enough for good maneuverability.

NUMBER OF SITES/UNITS

152 units. In July 1989 only 36 apartments were vacant, a comparatively small number.

LOCATION

Royal Palms is in north central Mesa. Two hospitals with large medical office buildings are less than two miles away. A Royal Palms shuttle bus makes almost daily runs to all types of shopping, banking, and various churches on Sundays. Unlike many retirement facilities in the Southwest, location and services make it possible to live nicely without a car. In addition, the nine-hole Royal Palms golf course is next door.

REQUIREMENTS/RESTRICTIONS

All residents must be 55 years or older. Children as well as other guests may visit, but after three days there is a $5.00-a-day charge. All guests must be registered with the management. Pets under 15 pounds are permitted, but a deposit is required

FEES

Longer term monthly lease rates are as follows: studio, $395; small one bedroom, $550; large one bedroom, $600; two bedroom, one bath, $700; two bedroom, two bath, $755; and the three bedroom is $1050. These prices are for unfurnished apartments. Furnished apartments may be available at higher rates. Various move-in specials are offered at different times. Short-term monthly prices for leases (three months) on furnished apartments are: studio, $900; one bedroom, $1305; and two bedroom, $1615. A few one- and two-month leases are available for furnished apartments, ranging from $1250 to $2315, depending on size available. Monthly rent includes housekeeping every other week, scheduled transportation, use of the clubhouse, and privileges at Royal Palms Golf Course. Dinner is served nightly, and residents are served in the dining room (in the clubhouse) for $3.95 per meal (a 20-meal punchcard for $79.00 is available for purchase). All apartments have a security call box which is monitored 24 hours a day.

AMENITIES

A large clubhouse/recreation center with dining room, pool and spa, beauty and barber shop, excellent transportation, movie nights in the clubhouse, and very good security highlight the amenities here. Golf privileges at the nine-hole Royal Palms Golf Course are included (greens fee additional).

REVIEWER'S NOTES

Royal Palms Retirement Park is well maintained in the common areas and grounds. The 152 apartments are housed in about 10 separate groupings, narrow but one-city-block long. Downstairs apartments have sliding glass doors in the rear of the apartment, many of them leading to the parking lot. Upstairs apartments have balconies in the rear. All hallways are open-air. This facility is especially nice for people living alone because of the security and scheduled transportation and outings. While anyone might appreciate the amenities here, older or less active people might find Royal Palms most attractive.

THE SPRINGS OF NORTH MESA

Rent

262 East Brown Road

Mesa, AZ 85201

(602) 844-9985

INDEPENDENT LIVING FACILITY

A planned apartment rental community for mature adults. Also caters to winter visitors. Established in 1986 and still owned jointly by VMS-Chicago and Pacific Scene—San Diego; managed by The Springs Management Company, which also manages two other communities in Arizona (east Mesa, Scottsdale) and four in California.

HOUSING TYPES AVAILABLE

One- and two-bedroom apartments in a two-story square building with a center courtyard. All apartments are one level and the one bedrooms are 600 sq ft; two bedrooms range from 816 to 1112 sq ft. The building has an elegant resort-type atmosphere with plush interior design and furnishings in a southwestern motif. The hallways are very wide and the apartments well laid out with wide doorways and big bathrooms. While not specifically catering to the disabled, accessibility is good and clearly the developers recognized the need for good, wide access.

NUMBER OF SITES/UNITS

174 apartments.

LOCATION

The Springs is located in north Mesa in an area that is at the heart of what Mesa has to offer. Excellent shopping malls, recreation (golf, YMCA), two major hospitals, a library, a major senior center, and Mesa Community College are all within a few minutes. You are within walking distance of where the Chicago Cubs hold spring training. This area can become congested, however. A car is not necessary due to the amenities provided at The Springs.

REQUIREMENTS/RESTRICTIONS

Minimum age 62. Pets are permitted.

FEES

One-bedroom unfurnished apartments rent for $975 per month; two-bedroom apartments for $1300 to $1400 for one person. There is a second person charge of $300. Services included in the monthly rent are two meals a day, weekly housekeeping, scheduled transportation, 24-hour staffing, social activities, cable television, and all utilities, except telephone. For winter visitors The Springs rents furnished one-bedroom apartments for $1800 to $1900 for one person; $300 additional for a second person. Services include those listed above except for choice of one meal a day (versus two).

AMENITIES

Apartments are spacious and have good storage, closet space, and balconies. Other amenities include emergency call systems in bedroom and bathroom, smoke detectors/sprinkler systems, and a fully enclosed environment where you can walk to dining and activities without going outside. Community amenities include a heated swimming pool, very elegant dining rooms, a library, a billiards and games area, a beauty and barber shop, scheduled transportation (The Spring's bus), and a very interesting "ice cream parlor" which is supplied by the management and residents use whenever they want an ice cream.

REVIEWER'S NOTES

The Springs is a very elegant community for those who are looking for resort-style living in a self-contained setting. The visitor feels very pampered because of the surroundings and atmosphere. For someone who is used to an elegant catered lifestyle this is an excellent choice. It is also excellent for winter visitors.

SUNLAND VILLAGE EAST

Buy

2150 South Farnsworth Drive

Mesa, AZ 85208

(602) 984-4999; (800) 777-7358

INDEPENDENT LIVING FACILITY

A master-planned active adult community in southeast Mesa. Established in 1985 by Farnsworth Development Company, builders of retirement communities since 1959.

HOUSING TYPES AVAILABLE

Single-family homes are available in seven different floor plans. The smallest model with two bedrooms and one bath is 1130 sq ft. The largest home available has three bedrooms, two baths, a separate family room, and a separate dining room, and measures 2131 sq ft. Regular lots are included in the list price. Golf course lots and large lots are available at additional cost. All are single level and the layout is basic. Condominiums are available with three different floor plans: one bedroom, two bath with 1010 sq ft; two bedroom, two bath with 1200 sq ft; and a larger two bedroom, two bath with 1320 sq ft.

NUMBER OF SITES/UNITS

Construction of new homes will be in five phases. Phases one and two are completed and phase three is well underway. Construction is expected to continue until 1995.

LOCATION

Sunland Village East has room to grow, yet is still within five miles of a hospital, physicians' offices, shopping, and other services. Superstition Freeway, which is less than two miles away, provides a quick route to the airport and downtown Phoenix. There are several golf courses nearby in addition to the one on site. There is no public transportation that serves this area, but Dial-a-Ride is available.

REQUIREMENTS/RESTRICTIONS

Minimum age 55; younger spouse must be at least 45. Pets are allowed in single-family homes. No pets in the condominiums.

FEES

Single-family homes range from $79,500 to $113,500. The average cost is about $90,000. Association fees are compulsory and run $158 per lot per year. Condominiums are classified either as "Garden," or "Golf" (overlooking the fairways). The floor plans for both are identical. Prices for garden condominiums range from $59,900 to $70,300. Golf condominiums range from $67,600 to $78,500. Monthly service fees range from $65 to $75 and include water and sewer, exterior maintenance, and association dues that provide access to recreational facilities. Golf course privileges may be purchased annually for $500 (couples $850) or each time you play: 18 holes, $14 or nine holes, $7.25.

AMENITIES

The multi-million dollar recreation center features: a 10,000-sq-ft auditorium, tennis courts, swimming pools, crafts rooms, card rooms, a billiards room, and several varieties of organized dancing. There is evening security with a cruising patrol car from 5:30 pm to 5:30 am. All the amenities listed are covered by the association fee.

REVIEWER'S NOTES

Sunland Village East offers retirement housing with a golf course at a very competitive price. Farnsworth Development Company has been building retirement communities in Mesa since 1959 and both Dreamland Villa and Sunland Village continue to thrive in a competitive market area. Resale homes in Farnsworth communities continue to bring sellers fair prices even with the currently "soft" market. While the homes at Sunland Village East are not very innovative architecturally (although not unattractive) they will probably outlive the more trendy models in other new developments. Sunland and other Farnsworth communities receive high marks from us where value is concerned.

SUNRISE VISTA

300 South Val Vista Drive

Mesa, AZ 85206

(602) 832-6214

INDEPENDENT LIVING FACILITY

A community of mobile homes (no RVs) in east central Mesa. A well-established park (over ten years old) controlled by the homeowners' association.

HOUSING TYPES AVAILABLE

Single- and double-wide mobile homes only; no park models or RVs. Most available housing is through resale or lease, but there are a few vacant spaces for new homes. Check with the office for information about leasing and resale of homes.

NUMBER OF SITES/UNITS

292 spaces located on several acres.

LOCATION

Sunrise Vista is located on Mesa's most popular and populated area for retirees. Medical facilities, shopping, banking, and golf courses are located well inside a five-mile radius. Since Sunrise Vista is south of Main Street, traffic is somewhat less heavy around the facility. Superstition Freeway provides easy access to Phoenix and the airport. Travel time to downtown Phoenix should average between 20 and 25 minutes. Dial-a-Ride is available to provide transportation if you do not care to drive.

REQUIREMENTS/RESTRICTIONS

Minimum age 55. Pets 20 pounds and under are welcome.

FEES

Monthly space rental for single-wide mobile homes is $254; $264 for double wides. This includes water, sewer, and trash pickup, as well as the use of recreation facilities. You may join the homeowners' association for $12.50 per year.

AMENITIES

Recreational activities include bingo, arts and crafts, potluck suppers, billiards, a putting green, and shuffleboard. There is also a community pool with a spa.

REVIEWER'S NOTES

Sunrise Vista is a quiet, well-maintained mobile home park. The convenient location and fairly small resident population may provide some individuals with enough activities to keep busy without being overwhelmed. The homeowners' association helps keep up with the residents' needs and fosters community spirit. A recommendation is given to those seeking a smaller park.

VIEW POINT RV AND GOLF RESORT

8700 East University Drive

Mesa, AZ 85207

(800) 822-4404; (602) 373-8700

INDEPENDENT LIVING FACILITY

An adult recreational vehicle (RV) resort with full hookups for your own vehicles. A recreation center and golf course are available.

HOUSING TYPES AVAILABLE

RV spaces for rent on a daily, weekly, monthly, or annual basis. Fairway spaces and spaces allowing pets are limited.

NUMBER OF SITES/UNITS

1350 spaces.

LOCATION

The northeast Mesa location is within easy driving distance (15 minutes) to shopping, medical services, churches, and entertainment. This particular area is still relatively uncongested and the view of the surrounding mountains is good.

REQUIREMENTS/RESTRICTIONS

Adults only. Advance deposits on monthly and yearly rentals. Pets limited to designated spaces.

FEES

The daily rate is $20; weekly, $110. Rates include electric, local telephone service (bring your own phone), and cable television. The monthly rate is $320; 6 months, $1695; and 12, $1875 and includes telephone and cable TV, but not electricity. All rates are before tax. Activities, water, sewer, and trash pickup are included with your rent. There is 24-hour security. Fairway spaces are an extra $200 per season. Green fees for residents range from

$4 to $6 for nine holes depending on the season. The yearly rate for a season's pass is $360 ($600 for a couple).

AMENITIES

Golf, tennis, two pools, four spas, a sauna, shuffleboard, horseshoe pits, billiard tables, picnic areas, 21 classroom/activity rooms, and a large dance floor are some of the amenities available to residents. The large main building has ample room for special groups or clubs (there are many) or other indoor activities. Instant phone service is available and is included in the rent. There is a concrete patio and drive on each space. The park has three large laundry and shower areas. Vehicle storage is available to all annual residents.

REVIEWER'S NOTES

The View Point RV and Golf Resort is large and modern. The management is helpful and the amenities are more plentiful than average. Summer occupancy is low—as with all RV parks in the area.

THE VILLAGE AT APACHE WELLS

5518 East Lindstrom Lane

Mesa, AZ 85205

(602) 830-2180

Rent

INDEPENDENT LIVING FACILITY

Adjacent to, but not affiliated with, Apache Wells golf resort. Owned by Sunbelt Savings.

HOUSING TYPES AVAILABLE

Apartments are very similar and range from 743 sq ft in the one bedroom to 1144 sq ft for the two-bedroom, two-bath model. In addition, there is a one bedroom with den with 950 sq ft. Individual apartments are on a single floor, but the complex is built on three floors. All doors open outdoors (there are no indoor hallways) and a patio or balcony is provided in all units. Some units have fireplaces.

NUMBER OF SITES/UNITS

124 rental units.

LOCATION

Northeast Mesa. The area is still relatively uncrowded with a view of the Superstition Mountains. Hospitals, shopping, and other services are within a five-mile radius. Transportation is by your own car or Dial-a-Ride (an independent reduced-rate private car service). There is no readily accessible public transportation. The freeway to Phoenix and the airport is about five miles away. All houses of worship except for a Jewish temple are also close by.

REQUIREMENTS/RESTRICTIONS

Minimum age 55; spouses under 55 are welcome. Visiting children are also welcome.

FEES

One-bedroom model rents for $445; one bedroom with den, $525; and two bedroom/two bath, $580 to $630.

AMENITIES

Facilities include a pool and spa, clubhouse, and exercise room. There are several public golf courses nearby, but not on site.

REVIEWER'S NOTES

This complex features a good location in terms of the proximity of undeveloped land with orange groves. It is adjacent to the Apache Wells golf resort retirement community, which is attractive and well maintained. Ground-level units have good handicapped accessibility, and bathrooms in most units are large enough to accommodate wheelchairs. Landscaping is sparse, with a small amount of lawn.

THE WELLS AT RED MOUNTAIN

5735 East McDowell

Mesa, AZ 85205

(602) 981-8806; (800) 359-3082

INDEPENDENT LIVING FACILITY

A planned adult community with manufactured homes and lots for sale. Established in 1987.

HOUSING TYPES AVAILABLE

Manufactured homes are available in your choice of seven floor plans or you can have a custom home in a wide variety of floorplans. Two models with one bedroom and one bath both have 640 sq ft. Five two-bedroom, two-bath models range from 800 to 1120 sq ft. There is one three-bedroom, two-bath model with 960 sq ft.

NUMBER OF SITES/UNITS

165 homes currently; 460 sites total.

LOCATION

Extreme northeast Mesa is still relatively uncrowded and offers mountain views. Medical facilities are just outside the five-mile radius. Shopping and other services are within a five-mile radius. Downtown Phoenix and the airport are about a 40-minute drive away. The facility is located on 38 acres.

REQUIREMENTS/RESTRICTIONS

Minimum age 40. Small pets allowed.

FEES

One-bedroom homes sell for $39,985 and $41,992. The two-bedroom models range from $50,760 to $62,253 and the three bedroom is priced at $59,025. Prices include lot and in-stallation/setup. The homeowners' fee is $37 monthly for a standard lot and $49.25 for a large lot. Water, sewer, garbage, and use of recreational facilities are included in the monthly fee.

AMENITIES

The Wells offers an 18-hole putting green, a million-dollar recreation center, tennis courts, and billiards. The facility has a security gate at the entrance. There are many scheduled activities and socials. Counted as an amenity would be the ability to own your own lot. This is not typical of many similar facilities.

REVIEWER'S NOTES

A good location and affordable housing makes The Wells an interesting option. The price may even make it possible to own as a second home. Homes are attractive inside and out. The streets are quite wide. Handicapped accessibility is only fair in common areas.

WHISPERING PINES OF MESA

35 West Brown Road

Mesa, AZ 85201

(602) 834-0600

Rent

Judy Murphy

INDEPENDENT LIVING FACILITY

A planned apartment rental community providing catered services for mature adults. Also caters to winter visitors. Established in 1985 as a Western Savings development. At the time of this review Western Savings was in bankruptcy and the property was for sale. Current management is under REM Corporation of Santa Anna. Caution is advised if considering this as a permanent residence due to the management situation.

HOUSING TYPES AVAILABLE

Studio, one-, and two-bedroom apartments in three-story buildings (with elevators). All apartments are one level and range in square footage from 383 to 825. All open to the outside. The apartments are spacious with good size bathrooms. The facility does not provide accessibility for the disabled.

NUMBER OF SITES/UNITS

255 apartments.

LOCATION

Whispering Pines is located in north Mesa in an excellent location very convenient to the airport, expressways, and the best of what Mesa has to offer. Excellent shopping, recreation, two major hospitals, a senior center, and the Chicago Cubs spring training are all nearby.

REQUIREMENTS/RESTRICTIONS

Minimum age 62—for couples, one spouse must be at least 62. Pets up to 20 pounds are allowed.

FEES

Studio unfurnished apartments—$455 to $540 per month; one bedroom, $530 to $660; two bedroom, $630 to $850, plus a 1 percent city tax. There is a second person charge of $50. Services included in the monthly rent are utilities (except telephone), weekly housekeeping, scheduled transportation, 24-hour staffing, cable television, and social activities. Meals are charged separately at $100 per month (three meals a day). There are separate rates for winter visitors (not available at the time of our visit).

AMENITIES

Apartments are spacious with good storage, balconies, and an emergency call system. Community amenities include a heated swimming pool, pleasant dining room, recreation room, library, exercise center, and hair styling salon. There is also a Whispering Pines bus, which provides residents with scheduled transportation (to physicians and shopping).

REVIEWER'S NOTES

Whispering Pines could be a very pleasant community for people seeking a middle class retirement, were it not for the management difficulties. The community also seems very well suited for winter visitors, who are less concerned over management.

CASA DEL RIO

Rent

12751 Plaza del Rio Boulevard

Peoria, AZ 85345

(602) 974-4700

INDEPENDENT LIVING FACILITY

A rental community for adults desiring assisted or catered living amenities. Part of a master-planned community that includes a health care campus with over 130 physicians and dentists, a skilled nursing facility, and the newly opened Freedom Plaza Lifecare Community. Casa del Rio is owned by Dr. Gries, Mrs. Harper, and other private individuals, and was established in 1984.

HOUSING TYPES AVAILABLE

One- and two-bedroom apartments available in three three-story elevator buildings. One of the buildings (a "preferred location") is connected to the main community/dining building so that residents do not have to walk outside. The other two buildings open to the outside. Apartments are available in four floor plans and range in size as follows: one-bedroom, 590 to 720 sq ft; two bedroom, 1000 to 1050 sq ft. Apartments are spacious and have washer/dryer units in the two-bedroom floor plan. All apartments have walk-in showers, guardrails in bathrooms, and emergency call systems. Accessibility for the disabled is good but there are some restrictions. A new development of 120 supervisory assisted living apartments is scheduled for completion in 1990. The lifecare community, Freedom Plaza, includes 350 apartments—for more information about this community call (602) 972-1776.

NUMBER OF SITES/UNITS

160 apartments.

LOCATION

Casa del Rio is located directly south of Sun City with very convenient access to Sun City services and amenities. Hospitals, physicians, shopping, churches, and local recreation are all within minutes. The Phoenix airport is about 40 minutes away in nonrush-hour traffic.

REQUIREMENTS/RESTRICTIONS

65 and older. Pets allowed.

FEES

Casa del Rio offers a package plan that includes meals, housekeeping, parking, and storage; or you can purchase these services individually. Monthly rental rates without the package plan are $790 to $890 for the one-bedroom unit and $1260 for the two bedroom. Included in these rates are all utilities (except phone), scheduled transportation, cable TV, social activities, and the use of all community amenities. There is an additional person charge of $40 per month. Costs of services purchased separately are as follows: meals run from $2 to $7.50 (breakfast and dinner); housekeeping, $14 to $16 per visit or $40 to $50 per month; covered parking, $15 per month; storage, $9 a month. The package plan rates are $945 to $1045 for the one bedroom and $1465 for the two bedroom. There is an additional person charge of $220 per month. For an apartment in a "preferred location," add $20 per month. Fees for furnished apartments for winter visitors run from $1250 to $1300 (one bedroom) and $2400 (two bedrooms). Amenities include weekly housekeeping, continental breakfast (other meals are extra), and the use of community facilities. Apartments may be rented for a minimum of three months.

AMENITIES

Community amenities include a swimming pool, whirlpool, putting green, shuffleboard court, library, card room, beauty/barber shop, an attractive dining room, and extensive social and recreational programs.

REVIEWER'S NOTES

Casa del Rio is a well-established rental community. As part of a planned community with extensive medical services nearby, as well as proximity to Sun City, Casa del Rio may be an excellent choice.

CASA DEL SOL

CASA DEL SOL #1

11411 North 91st Avenue

Peoria, AZ 85345

(602) 979-6913

CASA DEL SOL #2

10960 North 67th Avenue

Glendale, AZ 85304

(602) 979-6988

CASA DEL SOL #3

6960 West Peoria Avenue

Peoria, AZ 85345

(602) 979-6621

INDEPENDENT LIVING FACILITY

Three separate active facilities all composed of single- and double-wide mobile homes. First established in 1973. Operated by W.G. "Buzz" Kroger.

HOUSING TYPES AVAILABLE

Mobile homes individually owned on leased spaces. Resale homes and some new models available. Most are double-wide models with 700 to over 1000 sq ft. Many options are available and vary from home to home. All three parks are surrounded by block fences and have mature trees throughout and grassy common areas. There is a definite feeling of permanence quite different from the "trailer parks" of the past. All three have the same basic layout and appearance.

NUMBER OF SITES/UNITS

Casa del Sol #1, 246 spaces; Casa del Sol #2, about 250; and Casa del Sol #3, 235.

LOCATION

The three facilities are all in the northwest valley. Numbers 2 and 3 are almost next door to each other. Number 1 is less than five miles away to the west and borders Sun City. This area is convenient to three major hospitals, a large regional shopping mall, many golf courses, and other services. A car is highly desirable, as public transportation is spotty in this area. Travel time to downtown Phoenix and the airport averages between 35 and 45 minutes in off-peak hours.

REQUIREMENTS/RESTRICTIONS

Minimum age 55 for 80 percent of residents; 20 percent can be under 55. House pets (small dogs and cats) are allowed.

FEES

Home prices can range between $4500 and $40,000. Resale homes have carports, patios, and landscaping. Casa del Sol #1 has the lowest prices in general, but all three fall in a similar range. Monthly space rental is $225 to $300 and varies by size and park. Rental includes water, sewer, trash pickup, and the use of the recreation facilities.

AMENITIES

Casa del Sol resorts all have recreation centers that contain arts and crafts rooms, a swimming pool, putting greens, and lounge areas. Casa del Sol #1 has a recently remodeled recreation area. There are also large rooms with kitchens for community dinners, dances, and other special events. All streets have a posted 10-mile-per-hour speed limit; and because there are no through streets, there is little nonresident traffic. Each resort is separately managed.

REVIEWER'S NOTES

All of the Casa del Sol resorts are very clean, well maintained, and attractive. We were impressed with what we saw. We feel that all the communities are a good moderate priced alternative for individuals seeking an active retirement lifestyle in the northwest valley. These facilities can also make an ideal winter or second home.

DESERT AMETHYST

Rent

18170 North
91st Avenue
Peoria, AZ 85345
(602) 974-5848

INDEPENDENT LIVING FACILITY

A planned retirement full-service rental community. Established in 1988 by Netwest Development Corporation.

HOUSING TYPES AVAILABLE

One-bedroom, one-bath apartments are 760 sq ft; two bedroom, one bath, 905 sq ft; and two-bedroom, two-bath models with 1034 sq ft are available. All apartments are on one floor; second-floor apartments have vaulted ceilings. An assisted facility on site is presently under construction.

NUMBER OF SITES/UNITS

250 apartments.

LOCATION

Desert Amethyst has a Peoria address but is less than one mile from Sun City. All business, shopping and churches are conveniently located in the Sun City area. Downtown Phoenix and the airport are 30 miles away; the Black Canyon freeway, about 15 minutes. Rush-hour traffic is not much of a problem in this area. Westbrook Village is just across the road to the north. The two hospitals in Sun City, as well as many doctors' offices and specialty clinics, are within five miles.

REQUIREMENTS/RESTRICTIONS

Minimum age for all residents 62. Small pets are permitted, but a deposit is required.

FEES

Monthly rent including service fees begins at $1070 for the one-bedroom, one-bath apartment; $1230 for the two bedroom, one bath; and $1300 for the two bedroom, two bath. Each second person in the apartment is $250 additional per month. These rates include all utilities, continental breakfast and either lunch or dinner, bi-weekly housekeeping and linen service, 24-hour emergency call system and security, free laundry rooms, and scheduled transportation.

AMENITIES

There are many amenities included in the monthly fee. The dining room is elegant and has waitresses and waiters. The community social and recreation rooms are all in the main building and there is a pool. Although all apartments have indoor hallways, there are extensive outdoor walking paths for exercise. A cocktail lounge and ice cream parlor are on the premises. Room service for meals is available. Transportation is provided to shopping, banking, doctors' offices, and churches. Your own car is not a necessity.

REVIEWER'S NOTES

Desert Amethyst is a luxurious service- and amenity-oriented rental community. The apartments are light and well designed. The halls are very wide and well lit. The minimum age is 62 and there appeared to be a wide range of ages represented. It could be a good alternative to lifecare for those who wish to rent. A very attractive property.

SUN GROVE RESORT VILLAGE

Rent

10134 West Mohawk Lane

Peoria, AZ 85345

(602) 566-0745

INDEPENDENT LIVING FACILITY

An independent living rental community for mature adults desiring assisted or catered living services. Located adjacent to a skilled nursing facility. Established in 1986 by American Village Development. At the time of our visit, ownership/management was in the process of being transferred to Shurway Management Company.

HOUSING TYPES AVAILABLE

One-bedroom, one-bath to two-bedroom, two-bath apartments in a two-story development. One-bedroom units range from 505 to 836 sq ft; two bedrooms, 1058 to 1140. Apartments are all single level and open to the outside. Apartments are attractive and provide emergency call systems in rooms.

NUMBER OF SITES/UNITS

86 apartments completed; a second phase under consideration.

LOCATION

Sun Grove Resort Village is located just north of Sun City West in Peoria. Bordering the Sun City/Sun City West developments, it is in a less congested and somewhat more isolated area. Services and amenities such as a hospital, physicians' offices, shopping malls, churches, and entertainment can be found, however. Travel time to the Phoenix airport is about 45 minutes in off-peak hours.

REQUIREMENTS/RESTRICTIONS

No minimum age requirement, but most residents are retired. Pets are allowed.

FEES

One-bedroom, one-bath apartments rent for $675 per month; one-bedroom, one-and-a-half-bath apartments, $850; and two-bedroom units range from $1020 to $1115. The charge for an additional person is $60 per month. Fees include a utility allowance, scheduled transportation, 24-hour staffing, continental breakfast, parking, and the use of amenities. Covered parking is $15 per month extra. Housekeeping and meal services are optional. Housekeeping (once a week) for a one-bedroom unit is $50 per month; once every other week, $25 per month. Dinner is optional at $142.50 per month or $6.00 daily.

AMENITIES

The community includes an elegant dining room, clubhouse, library/reading room, billiards/card room, exercise room, arts and crafts, a swimming pool, shuffleboard courts, and a putting green.

REVIEWER'S NOTES

For someone who is looking for a small, pleasant community in a comfortable environment, this could be a good choice.

WESTBROOK VILLAGE

Buy

9721 West Rockwood Drive

Peoria, AZ 85345

(602) 933-0181; (800) 892-2838;

(602) 939-4799 (Village Square Condo)

INDEPENDENT LIVING FACILITY

A planned community for mature adults desiring an active, country-club-style setting. Established in 1982 by UDC Homes, who continue to develop and manage the community today.

HOUSING TYPES AVAILABLE

Single-family homes, patio homes, manor homes, and condominiums are available. Most homes have two bedrooms and two baths; there are also three-bedroom, two-bath models. Square footage ranges from 1318 to 2264. Westbrook Village has 17 models to choose from. Manor homes are single-family detached units with smaller lots; patio homes are attached. The homes are all single level, many with vaulted ceilings and mission tile roofing. Resales are also available. The condominiums, which have one and two bedrooms, are built in three-story buildings, each with 24 units. The one-bedroom units are about 800 sq ft; the two bedroom about 1200. The condominiums (Village Square) are located in the center of the community overlooking the golf course.

NUMBER OF SITES/UNITS

Currently 2700 residents with 1800 homes sold—90 percent of the current development. Plans include a new phase of similar size opening next year.

LOCATION

Westbrook Village is located in the northwest valley and is very near Sun City. This area is developing rapidly but is still less congested than other parts of the valley. Hospitals, physicians' offices, shopping, and churches are within a five-mile radius. A new shopping center is being developed nearby. Westbrook is about 35 minutes from downtown Phoenix; 45 minutes from the Phoenix airport in off-peak hours.

REQUIREMENTS/RESTRICTIONS

One member of the family must be at least 55.

FEES

New single-family homes with two bedrooms and two baths begin at $81,900 and climb from $112,900 to $128,900 for the largest two-bedroom/den and three-bedroom homes. Patio homes range from $78,900 to $84,400. Manor homes range from $98,300 to $106,600. Condominiums range from $60,500 to $94,400; penthouses from $179,900. Homeowners' fees are $260 per year per household and include use of all recreational facilities (except golf) as well as landscaping maintenance of common areas. Manor home and patio homeowners also pay a monthly fee of about $100 for landscaping of individual lots and maintenance of amenities. Condominium owners pay an association fee of $120 per month, which includes water, sewer, trash pickup, and the use of recreational facilities (except golf). Golf membership fees are $800 for one person; $1400 for a couple. Daily green fees are $12 to $26 depending on the time of year. Nonresidents can join—fees are substantially higher.

AMENITIES

The community is beautifully landscaped with an 18-hole golf course, tennis courts, and an elegant country club. An impressive recreation center offers an olympic-size pool, exercise facilities, a craft center, and a multitude of meeting and game rooms. There is also a multi-purpose auditorium.

REVIEWER'S NOTES

Westbrook Village is an elegant community for active adults who are looking for a country-club-type setting. This is clearly an active community for people who like recreational and social amenities. This reviewer visited during the summer, when people were outdoors bicycling, playing golf, or swimming. The homes are spacious with large windows. Many have high ceilings, which gives an open feeling.

AHWATUKEE

11022 South 51st Street

Phoenix, AZ 85044

Center Court (new homes), (602) 893-2646;

Resales, (602) 893-3131;

Realty Executives, (602) 893-2888

Buy

INDEPENDENT LIVING FACILITY

A planned community that contains separate retirement and family developments. Established in 1971 and developed by The Presley Companies.

HOUSING TYPES AVAILABLE

Single-family homes and some apartments in a large variety of sizes and models built over a 16-year period. New homes were expected to be sold out by the end of 1989. At the time of our visit there were only 29 new model homes available at the new Center Court development. There were four models to choose from—two single level and two double level, with square footage ranging from 1195 to 1698. Resales are available. Some very upscale custom development is also available. The community is unique in that it features retirement, adult, and family developments.

NUMBER OF SITES/UNITS

Over 6000 homes; over 90 percent completed.

LOCATION

Ahwatukee is located in south Phoenix just off I-10. It is very convenient to the Phoenix airport, the Tempe-Mesa area, and southern parts of Phoenix. Downtown Phoenix is 30 to 45 minutes away depending on traffic. Hospitals, doctors' offices, supermarkets, shopping, and churches are all within a five-mile radius. The setting is attractive with mountain views; it is somewhat secluded and private.

REQUIREMENTS/RESTRICTIONS

In retirement areas one member (owner) must be 55 or over. Pets allowed.

FEES

New single-family homes in the Center Court development range from $85,100 to $107,300. Resales start in the $70,000 range and custom homes cost as much as $140,000. Owners pay annual common area fees of about $55 per year per family. Recreation fees (optional) are $1000 to $1750 per year for golf (family membership), $180 per year for swimming (family), and $122 per year for the use of the recreation center (per person).

AMENITIES

The new homes we saw were attractive, featuring cathedral ceilings and large open kitchens. A number of the homes are two floor, which is unusual for Arizona. Since most of the housing is resale, there are a lot of different options available. Ahwatukee has two 18-hole golf courses, tennis courts, and a number of recreation areas for each separate development, with swimming pools and Jacuzzi, an exercise room, bowling, arts and crafts, shuffleboard, and other activities.

REVIEWER'S NOTES

For active adults who are looking for a retirement community nestled in with adult and family communities, this is an ideal choice. Ahwatukee is well established, and we found the setting attractive.

BOULDER RIDGE

2233 East Behrend Drive

Phoenix, AZ 85024

(602) 569-1777; (602) 934-5254

(Busbee's Sales)

INDEPENDENT LIVING FACILITY

A community of manufactured (mobile) homes. Established in 1981; Hillsboro Properties, owner/operator.

HOUSING TYPES AVAILABLE

Individually owned manufactured mobile homes. The homes, available from different manufacturers, vary in size, price, and design. Popular models range in size from under 1000 to 1600 sq ft. Manufactured homes can be customized in much the same way as conventional homes, so your options are many. The interiors of these homes are virtually the same as a conventional home. They are attractive outside and inside and do not give the impression of being "transitory." Periodically there are resale homes available through the development.

NUMBER OF SITES/UNITS

Approximately 200. There are still open lots for lease.

LOCATION

Boulder Ridge is located in north central Phoenix. It lies within the city limits but is very close to unincorporated and undeveloped land. The name comes from its location, which is at the foot of a small mountain covered with boulders. Many of the boulders have been left on community land, and the home sites are designed around them. The community is hidden from view from the main road and is quite unique and attractive. Travel time to the airport and downtown Phoenix is about 30 minutes.

REQUIREMENTS/RESTRICTIONS

Age 55 and over. Small pets up to 15 pounds. Children may visit.

FEES

Homes may be purchased from $28,000 to over $65,000 new. Monthly leases run from $170 to $250 depending on lot size and location. Fees cover the use of the recreational facilities, as well as security and maintenance for common areas.

AMENITIES

An electronic gate has been installed at the entrance. Residents have a magnetic card to operate it, and there is a phone for visitors to use to be admitted by the resident they are visiting. The gate is closed at sundown. Recreational facilities consist of a clubhouse, two pools in different locations, and tennis courts. Shopping, churches, and medical facilities are within a five-mile radius. Public buses are about a 10-minute walk, so it is advisable to have your own car.

REVIEWER'S NOTES

Boulder Ridge is uniquely and naturally landscaped and is obscured from traffic by a mountain. It truly gives the impression that it is far from the city. The homes are nice and well kept. Many of the residents still work so it has a younger and more active atmosphere. Manufactured homes in this setting can save you money and still be pleasant and comfortable.

FELLOWSHIP SQUARE

Rent

2002 West Sunnyside Drive

Phoenix, AZ 85071-3210

(602) 943-1800

INDEPENDENT LIVING FACILITY

Fellowship Square is located in north central Phoenix and provides rental housing in a Christian setting. Established by the Christian Churches of Arizona.

HOUSING TYPES AVAILABLE

Apartments in a multi-story building are available in three different floor plans. The smallest unit is a one bedroom with 614 sq ft. Two-bedroom, two-bath models have either 878 or 1020 sq ft. Each of the three models has a standard kitchen, walk-in closet, and balcony with an enclosed storage area. Hallways are interior and there are elevators to upper floors. Garden home duplexes are single-level, white stucco units. Two models are available. Both have two bedrooms and two baths and 949 or 1097 sq ft. These homes have covered carports, walk-in closets, and have a high block wall in the rear blocking the view from the street. There is a nursing care center on site.

NUMBER OF SITES/UNITS

Approximately 28 garden homes and over 100 apartments.

LOCATION

Fellowship Square is located in north central Phoenix near the Black Canyon Freeway. This area is known as Moon Valley because of the nearby mountains, which resemble a lunar landscape with craters. Well within a five-mile radius are several hospitals, a major regional mall, supermarkets, banks, and golf courses. Travel time to the airport averages around 20 minutes. Public transportation (bus) stops on the corner of this facility.

REQUIREMENTS/RESTRICTIONS

Minimum age 62. Small pets allowed.

FEES

Monthly price for the one-bedroom apartment is $750; small two bedroom, $1165; and large two bedroom, $1495. Duplexes are priced at $1645. The garden duplexes run $1645 and $1995. Monthly rent includes utilities, 25 meals, biweekly housekeeping, and maintenance. Prices are for one person; add $250 for a second person.

AMENITIES

Fellowship Square provides scheduled transportation to supermarkets, malls, and medical facilities. Social, recreational, and cultural activities are regularly scheduled. There is a pool and exercise room for working out. Residents will have priority status at the care center if needed.

REVIEWER'S NOTES

This community is quite attractive for several reasons—first, the buildings and grounds are pleasing to the eye. If a Christian environment is important to you, Fellowship Square offers this without a buy-in or endowment. We found the garden duplexes especially nice. The location is another plus, as it is more centrally located than similar facilities in Mesa and Sun City.

FRIENDLY VILLAGE OF ORANGEWOOD

2650 West Union Hills Drive

Phoenix, AZ 85027

(602) 869-7498

INDEPENDENT LIVING FACILITY

A quiet adult mobile home community in north Phoenix with resident managers.

HOUSING TYPES AVAILABLE

Mobile homes are individually owned and set up on leased lots. Double-wide and single-wide mobiles are permitted. There are homes for resale around the park as well as some spaces available for new homes. A variety of sizes and floor plans exist, but most common is a home with two bedrooms and one bath.

NUMBER OF SITES/UNITS

384 spaces.

LOCATION

Friendly Village is located in the extreme north section of Phoenix. The area is growing rapidly, but is still much less congested than the Sun City or east Mesa areas. New medical facilities (hospitals and clinics) have recently opened in this area along with shopping and other services. Travel time to downtown Phoenix and the airport is around 45 minutes. Sun City is about six miles to the west. Interstate 17 is less than five minutes away.

REQUIREMENTS/RESTRICTIONS

Adults only. Small pets allowed. Homes can be 12, 14, or 16 feet wide and a maximum of 61 feet long.

FEES

Resale homes typically range from $12,000 to $35,000. New models run about $5000 to $10,000 more, not including transport and setup charges. Spaces cost an average of $285 per month. Included in this fee is water, sewer, and trash collection. Resale homes are usually for sale by the owner. A drive through the park if you are in the area will usually yield a fair selection of homes on the market. The office may be able to direct you to individuals with homes for sale if you are not able to visit the park yourself. However, the office does not function as a sales office.

AMENITIES

Recreational facilities include a private golf course, swimming pools, a clubhouse with card and game rooms, and shuffleboard courts. The clubhouse hosts many community events, and regularly scheduled bingo games are very popular. The park is located in a mature citrus grove, making the setting quite green (the fruit is also delicious).

REVIEWER'S NOTES

Friendly Village of Orangewood is a quiet and—yes—friendly mobile home community. Outstanding features were the citrus trees in everyone's yard and the feeling of community spirit and pride expressed by the residents. A good number of residents do leave for cooler parts of the country during the summer, but there are also quite a few that remain. The lower purchase price and upkeep costs of a mobile home enable many people to maintain another home (or an RV) and spend winters and summers in ideal climates.

OLIVE GROVE RETIREMENT VILLAGE

Rent

3014 East Indian School Road

Phoenix, AZ 85016

(602) 957-7021

INDEPENDENT LIVING FACILITY

A rental retirement community for mature adults needing catered or assisted living services. Established in 1980; owned and managed for the last two years by Hillhaven, which owns/manages other communities nationwide.

HOUSING TYPES AVAILABLE

Rooms and suites are laid out hotel style—either furnished or unfurnished—in a three-story elevator "T"-shaped building. The rooms and suites are available in three plans: private room, mini-suite, and two-room suite (like a one bedroom). The rooms have bathrooms but no kitchens. All have balconies or patios. The apartments all open inward to wide corridors—you do not need to go outside to get to dining or other activities.

NUMBER OF SITES/UNITS

100 rooms/suites.

LOCATION

Olive Grove is located on Indian School Road just west of 32nd Street in east central Phoenix. The area is very convenient to downtown Phoenix, Phoenix airport, and Scottsdale. Hospitals, doctors, shopping (including a major shopping center near the Arizona Biltmore), churches, and recreation facilities are all nearby. The area can become congested but Olive Grove provides scheduled transportation so a car is not a necessity.

REQUIREMENTS/RESTRICTIONS

Minimum age 55. No pets.

FEES

The standard suite (private room) rents for $795 per month; deluxe suite, $995 per month; and the two-room suite, $1675 per month for one person. Furnished and unfurnished units are the same price. There is an additional person charge of $250 per month. Services included in the monthly fee are three meals a day, 24-hour staffing, social activities, daily housekeeping service and linens, use of all community services, and utilities (except phone). Olive Grove also provides additional assisted living services for $300 to $500 per month depending on personal needs. These include assistance in daily living such as bathing, medication reminders, and dressing.

AMENITIES

The community offers a swimming pool and Jacuzzi, attractive area for walking, beauty/barber shop, billiards room, and recreational and social activities. Assisted living services are stressed and emphasis is placed on amenities in this area.

REVIEWER'S NOTES

Olive Grove is a community in transition under the relatively new ownership of Hillhaven. During our visit we learned that Hillhaven plans to stress assisted living services and add or upgrade staffing and services. This will be a good community for people requiring more assisted living services, depending upon the outcome of Hillhaven's plans.

ORANGEWOOD

Buy

7550 North 16th Street

Phoenix, AZ 85020

(602) 944-4455

INDEPENDENT LIVING FACILITY

A "campus"-style community with housing ranging from independent living apartments to a skilled nursing facility. Established in 1963 and still owned and operated by American Baptist Homes of the West.

HOUSING TYPES AVAILABLE

Apartments available in five floor plans. Studio apartments are without kitchen and provide 316 sq ft. Two models of one-bedroom, one-bath apartments are either 475 or 540 sq ft. The two-bedroom, one-bath model is 660 sq ft; and the two bedroom, two bath, 1129 sq ft. All apartments have patios; patios in some models are enclosed. There is a security call system in each apartment. The whole community occupies 20 acres, and all apartments are single level. The connecting hallways are open, but all are covered.

NUMBER OF SITES/UNITS

206 apartments.

LOCATION

Orangewood is in north central Phoenix. It is across the street from the five star Pointe Resort at the base of Squaw Peak mountains. All services are within a five-mile radius, including the airport.

REQUIREMENTS/RESTRICTIONS

Minimum age 62. Small pets are permitted.

FEES

Entrance fees (endowments) are assessed at the time of entrance. These fees are nonrefundable (except with residency of not more than five years) and entitle residents to keep their apartments for as long as they want or are able to. There is also a monthly services fee. Apartments can be obtained starting at $19,200 for a studio. The two one-bedroom, one-bath models range from $37,800 to $46,800. Two bedroom with one bath starts at $58,200; and the two bedroom, two bath ranges from $84,200 to $88,200. The prices listed are for single occupancy. The price is higher for two persons. Monthly fees are based both on apartment size and the number of occupants. A studio apartment with one occupant is $564; a small one bedroom, $657 (single), or $959 (double); a two bedroom, one bath, $751 (single), or $1023 (double); and a deluxe two bedroom, two bath, $1199 (double). The monthly fee provides one meal daily, utilities, pool, facilities, local transportation, and a security program. It also includes weekly maid and laundry service (linens).

AMENITIES

Amenities are included in the monthly service fee. The 64-bed skilled nursing center admits only residents, and Orangewood has several "in-house" financial plans to provide insurance for nursing home stays. Twenty studio apartments designated for assisted living are for residents who may need help with personal care (nonmedical) but wish to remain independent.

REVIEWER'S NOTES

Orangewood is attractive and well maintained even after more than 25 years. The apartments have safety features in the bathrooms and higher than average ceilings. The grounds are green and well kept. The staff and residents seemed happy to be there. This is another "endowment" community that may merit further consideration. Vacancies do exist but both Orangewood and Glencroft have higher occupancy rates than similar deeded ownership or rental communities. If Orangewood meets most of your requirements, it may be worth contacting for more detailed information.

PARADISE PEAK WEST

3901 East Pinnacle Peak Road

Phoenix, AZ 85024

(602) 946-2299

INDEPENDENT LIVING FACILITY

An adult mobile (manufactured) home community. Established in 1985, developed, owned, and managed by Sierra National Corporation of Phoenix.

HOUSING TYPES AVAILABLE

Manufactured mobile homes are available for individual purchase in a variety of sizes, designs, and price ranges. The sales office represents the Fleetwood Company, but you may choose another manufacturer if you prefer. The general range of sizes is 700 to 1700 sq ft.

NUMBER OF SITES/UNITS

413 lots; about 240 are still available for new homes.

LOCATION

Paradise Peak West is in far northeast Phoenix, near the north Scottsdale and Paradise Valley areas. Since the surrounding area is as yet undeveloped, there is plenty of wide open space. Shopping, medical, banking, and other services are within an eight-mile radius. Construction plans for some of these businesses and services are in the early stages. When completed, banking and a supermarket will be about three miles away. A car is necessary. Advantages to this location are its scenic views and quiet.

REQUIREMENTS/RESTRICTIONS

Age 55 and over. Small pets allowed, but a deposit is required.

FEES

Homes purchased from the developer begin at $22,500 and can exceed $60,000 The price of these homes includes setup, carport, and patio. You may purchase from other manufacturers at similar prices, but expect to pay an additional $8000 for setup in the development. Individual lots rent for $250 and $290 (golf course and premium lots) monthly. The rent includes water and sewer, trash pickup, a 24-hour security guard at the gate, and unlimited use of the nine-hole golf course.

AMENITIES

Among the amenities is an activity center designed by Frank Lloyd Wright, with card rooms, game rooms, a billiard room, a pro shop, and a lounge. Residents may use the nine-hole golf course without paying a fee. There is also a lighted tennis court, a heated pool, and a Jacuzzi. The staffed security gate provides 24-hour service.

REVIEWER'S NOTES

Paradise Peak West has many attractive features but is too far away from basic services to be appealing to everybody. It is perfect for those seeking a feeling of space and an escape from the urban rush. Most urban conveniences can be reached in 15 minutes. The cost of homes and golf course usage are pluses.

PARADISE VALLEY ESTATES

11645 North 25th Place

Phoenix, AZ 85028

(602) 482-7100

Buy

INDEPENDENT LIVING FACILITY

An endowment community. Established in 1985, Paradise Valley Estates is a nonprofit corporation affiliated with Arizona Baptist Retirement Services and sponsored by the Arizona's Baptist Convention.

HOUSING TYPES AVAILABLE

One- and two-bedroom apartments are available in five two-story elevator buildings. Apartments all open outward and are all single level. One-bedroom apartments are 682 sq ft; one-bedroom with den and two-bedroom apartments are 877 sq ft. All apartments except the newest have patios or balconies. The newer apartments are the same size but the patios/balconies have been eliminated to provide additional inside living space. The apartments themselves, called "garden homes," are among some of the nicest we have seen. They are spacious with separate dining areas. Second-floor apartments have vaulted ceilings. All have emergency call systems, sprinklers, and security systems. Each apartment has a bathroom with walk-in shower.

NUMBER OF SITES/UNITS

100 apartments.

LOCATION

Paradise Valley Estates is located in an attractive residential section of north Phoenix in the west Paradise Valley area. The community is adjacent to Southwestern Bible College and Paradise Valley Retirement Center, a HUD-subsidized 120-apartment retirement community. The location is excellent in that hospitals, physicians' offices, shopping, churches, and recreation are nearby and you are close to everything Phoenix has to offer.

This area is also somewhat less congested than other parts of Phoenix. The Phoenix airport is about 30 minutes away in nonrush-hour traffic.

REQUIREMENTS/RESTRICTIONS

Minimum age is 60 (one member of couple). Small pets allowed.

FEES

Endowment fees for one-bedroom apartments range from $64,900 to $65,900; for two bedroom, from $74,900 to $75,900. There is no additional charge for a second person or covered parking. The monthly service fee for the apartments (all sizes) is $169 and covers maintenance, common area charges, 24-hour security, and the use of all community facilities. Utilities are additional. Regarding endowment fees, the community offers two options for the return of a portion of your equity. The first option is a straight 81 percent equity plan; the second option involves an equity prorated according to your age and includes a share of profit upon resale if applicable. Remember that as with most of these types of communities your equity is returned after resale.

AMENITIES

The community offers a recreation center with crafts, a large swimming pool, large auditorium, shuffleboard court, library, scheduled transportation, beauty and barber shop, and a library. The community is very nicely laid out with landscaped walkways and "old fashioned" courtyards.

REVIEWER'S NOTES

Paradise Valley Estates is one of the smaller endowment communities we visited. The community is very attractive with some of the nicest apartments we have seen anywhere. The location near Paradise Valley is also a plus.

PHOENIX MANOR

2636 North 41st Avenue

Phoenix, AZ 85009

(602) 272-0496

Rent

Peggy Williams, Manager

INDEPENDENT LIVING FACILITY

A planned rental community for mature adults desiring an active lifestyle setting. Established and owned since 1962 by a private owner.

HOUSING TYPES AVAILABLE

Studio, one-bedroom, and two-bedroom apartments available in five models. The apartments look more like patio homes/townhouses in that most are single level and spread out over a 25-acre development with 4 to 12 apartments in each building. Apartments range from approximately 375 to over 700 sq ft and have patios or balconies. The apartments are spacious with lots of closet space. All apartments open to outside walkways.

NUMBER OF SITES/UNITS

450 apartments: 58 studios, 236 one bedrooms, and 156 two bedrooms.

LOCATION

Phoenix Manor is located in west central Phoenix in an older, established part of the city. Hospitals, doctors' offices, shopping, churches, and recreation are all nearby. The community, which is set back from the main Thomas Road artery, is fairly private.

REQUIREMENTS/RESTRICTIONS

Minimum age 50; no pets allowed.

FEES

Studio unfurnished apartments rent for $330 per month (plus 1.2 percent tax), one-bedroom units for $375, and two bedroom for $415 to $463 per month. These monthly rental fees include all utilities (except cable and telephone) and use of all community facilities. Parking is available for an additional $6 to 8 per month.

AMENITIES

Phoenix Manor stresses amenities for active, mature adults including two swimming pools and a Jacuzzi, two clubhouses, and a very extensive program of activities and clubs. The Manor also emphasizes that it provides a "maintenance-free" lifestyle: all maintenance of the apartments, landscaping, and community is handled by full-time staff.

REVIEWER'S NOTES

Phoenix Manor is an attractive rental community for active, mature adults. The term "Manor" really does not describe the feeling of this community. It looks much more like a community of homes, with mostly single-level units and lots of space. It has a very unpretentious and pleasant feeling to it. People seem to enjoy living there.

PHOENIX MOUNTAIN VILLA

13240 North Tatum Boulevard

Phoenix, AZ 85032

(602) 953-3600

Rent   **Ruth Kent Grina, Retirement Counselor**

INDEPENDENT LIVING FACILITY

A retirement apartment center including supervisory care and skilled nursing facilities. The nursing facility opened in 1980, and the independent living apartments opened in 1986. Phoenix Mountain Villa was developed and is still owned privately.

HOUSING TYPES AVAILABLE

Apartments designed for independent living are available in five different floor plans. The studio apartment has 420 sq ft, the one-bedroom suite, 580. Three different two-bedroom models (one with two baths) are 791, 861, and 908 sq ft in size. All apartments have either enclosed patios or balconies and all walkways/hallways are enclosed. The complex is on three floors, with individual units on a single floor. The apartments are well designed for optimum use of space, and storage areas are adequate. Kitchens are small, but there is little need for more room because meals are included in the rent. There are upgraded features such as carpet and cabinets.

NUMBER OF SITES/UNITS

109 independent living apartments, 30 apartments designed for supervisory care, and 127 beds in the skilled nursing facility.

LOCATION

The community is located in northeast Phoenix/Paradise Valley, an area noted for its elegant homes, designer shops, and mountain views. All services are within a five-mile radius, and a major shopping center is a block away. Traffic from the shopping center is not a problem because the facility is not on a main thoroughfare. The immediate area surrounding the facility is newly built and comprised of townhouses and condominiums.

REQUIREMENTS/RESTRICTIONS

No specific age requirement. Small pets are permitted.

FEES

Monthly rent begins at $950 for the studio model; one bedroom, $1250; two bedrooms, $1450, $1550, and $1650 depending on size. Charge for an additional person is $250 per month. In addition to the two daily meals (served restaurant style) the rent includes utilities, all interior and exterior maintenance, weekly maid service, 24-hour emergency call system, 24-hour security, scheduled transportation, recreational programs, and use of the pool.

AMENITIES

All the amenities listed above are covered by the monthly rent.

REVIEWER'S NOTES

Paradise Mountain Villa is a good option for those looking for security and a full range of amenities and services in an elegant setting. It appears to cater to the less physically active retiree but has a good selection of scheduled events and activities. The licensed and certified nursing center on site will be a comfort to some. The surrounding area is attractive and services are quite accessible.

PHOENIX NORTH MOBILE HOME COMMUNITY

17825 North 7th Street

Phoenix, AZ

(602) 992-4116

INDEPENDENT LIVING FACILITY

A community of mobile homes in north central Phoenix. An established park.

HOUSING TYPES AVAILABLE

Mobile homes, both single- and double-wide, individually owned on leased lots. As with other mobile home communities, a variety of sizes and floor plans exist.

NUMBER OF SITES/UNITS

135 spaces.

LOCATION

Phoenix North is within a five-mile radius of several hospitals, major shopping centers, golf courses, and a wide range of other services and businesses. Many of the small mountains in this area are designated preserves and by law will not be developed. This area is also noted for its luxury home developments. It is attractive not only because of the mountains but also because travel time to central Phoenix and the airport is under 30 minutes. Turf Paradise (horse racing) is popular with many retirees in the area and is only 10 minutes away from this community.

REQUIREMENTS/RESTRICTIONS

Minimum age 55. Pets under 20 pounds permitted.

FEES

Frequently there are several homes for sale in this park. Typically prices range from the mid-teens to around $40,000. Monthly rental for spaces is $238 to $248 and includes water, sewer, and trash collection.

AMENITIES

There is a community pool and Jacuzzi for residents as well as a community clubhouse. Community-sponsored events and activities occur on a regular basis—more frequently during winter months.

REVIEWER'S NOTES

Phoenix North Mobile Home Community appears to be clean and quiet. While this is not one of the larger parks, it is in an excellent location and is on the city of Phoenix bus line. It may be a good choice for a "winter" home as well as a permanent home.

THE FORUM-PUEBLO NORTE

Buy

7090 East Mescal
Street
Scottsdale, AZ
85254
(602) 948-3990

INDEPENDENT LIVING FACILITY

A lifecare community established in 1985 by the Adventist Church. Acquired in July 1988 by Forum Lifecare, Inc. and now managed by The Forum Group, Inc., Indianapolis. This same company operates retirement communities in Peoria (The Forum at Desert Harbor) and Tucson (The Forum at Tucson), Arizona; and in Albuquerque, New Mexico (The Montebello on Academy, reviewed in this volume).

HOUSING TYPES AVAILABLE

Studio, one- and two-bedroom apartments, and one- and two-bedroom villas are available. Apartments are located in a two-story complex. Studio apartments are 400 sq ft; one bedroom, 668; two bedrooms, from 875 to 1336. The villas start with one-bedroom units at 692 sq ft; two bedrooms, from 962 to 1228.

NUMBER OF SITES/UNITS

140 Apartments, 37 villas; an on site licensed health center/nursing care facility.

LOCATION

The Forum is located in north Scottsdale in an urban area to the east of Paradise Valley. The area is very convenient to major services and amenities and not as congested as central Scottsdale. Major hospitals are nearby—the Mayo Clinic is six miles away—and churches, shopping, and recreational activities abound. The community is about 35 minutes from the Phoenix airport.

REQUIREMENTS/RESTRICTIONS

Minimum age 62 (spouse can be younger); pets are allowed depending on size.

FEES

This is a lifecare community in which a resident pays an initial membership fee and then monthly fees in return for housing, assisted living services, other amenities, and certain nursing care guarantees for life. In addition to a rental option and "Lifecare Estate Plan," The Forum also offers a program called "Lifecare with Equity," which allows refunds of your initial membership fee. The initial membership fee for a studio apartment is $65,000; for a one bedroom, $98,500; a one-bedroom villa, $105,000; a two-bedroom villa, $160,000-$175,000. The monthly fee for a studio is $750; for a one bedroom, $875-$895; for a two-bedroom apartment or villa, $975-$1095. The charge for an additional person is $450 per month. These fees include one meal per day, all utilities, local telephone, weekly housekeeping, scheduled transportation, 24-hour staffing, and use of community amenities.

AMENITIES

Community amenities include a swimming pool, elegant dining room, full-time program/activities director, library, craft room, and game rooms.

REVIEWER'S NOTES

An attractive lifecare community in an excellent location. The feeling is elegant but not overwhelming. This reviewer had some questions about the layout for people requiring assisted living services but not nursing care. For example, the apartments open to the outside and can be quite a distance from the main facility. People use carts to get around and there is a pickup service. The staff seemed very professional.

SCOTTSDALE SHADOWS

Buy

7870 East Camelback Road

Scottsdale, AZ 85251

(602) 994-8066

INDEPENDENT LIVING FACILITY

A planned condominium community for adults. Established in 1974 by EDI; current units for sale owned by Carlsdale Consortium, Carlsbad, New Mexico. Internal management hired by the homeowners' association.

HOUSING TYPES AVAILABLE

One-bedroom, one-and-a-half bath to three-bedroom, three-bath new condominiums, plus resales, available in four- to seven-story high-rise, elevator buildings. The entire complex consists of 13 buildings. One-bedroom units range from 860 to 1064 sq ft; two bedrooms, from 1208 to 1578; three bedrooms, 1976 to 2140. All units are single level with balconies. The buildings have sprinkler and fire alarm systems. Apartments are spacious with big kitchens. Accessibility for the disabled is available in only one building.

NUMBER OF SITES/UNITS

837 units in 13 buildings.

LOCATION

Scottsdale Shadows is located in central Scottsdale in an attractive urban area convenient to all types of services and amenities. The city of Scottsdale is known for its exclusivity, and the Shadows is near all that Scottsdale has to offer. Also within a five-mile radius are numerous physicians' offices, hospitals, churches, and temples, as well as entertainment. It is approximately 25 minutes from the Phoenix airport.

REQUIREMENTS/RESTRICTIONS

Minimum age recommended is 40. There are no pets allowed (this rule is strictly enforced).

FEES

Condominiums: one-bedroom units start at $62,000; two bedrooms at $78,000; and three bedrooms at $148,000. Also included in these prices are one parking space (underground-enclosed) and one storage room. Monthly condominium dues, which include air conditioning, heat, water, trash pickup, and all amenities, range from $198 per month (one bedroom) to $454-$492 (three bedrooms). Yearly property taxes start at $363 per year (one bedroom) to $859 (three bedrooms). The Shadows is interested in winter visitors and offers about 50 winter rentals each year for a minimum of four months. Rates vary. For more information call (602) 994-8066.

AMENITIES

Scottsdale Shadows offers a variety of amenities and services. The community is self-contained. Security services at the front entrance monitor all people entering or leaving the community. Amenities include a private nine-hole golf course, three tennis courts, three swimming pools, and a large clubhouse. The Shadows stresses that it has a full-time activities director and that activities, social events, and trips abound throughout the year.

REVIEWER'S NOTES

Scottsdale Shadows is a condominium community for those who are looking for urban, high-rise living with a wide choice of social activities. The community is appealing and well maintained. To this reviewer it had the closest feeling to an east coast community that he had experienced. Definitely worth visiting if you like this type of setting.

SCOTTSDALE VILLAGE SQUARE

Rent

2620 North 68th Street

Scottsdale, AZ 85257

(602) 946-6571

INDEPENDENT LIVING FACILITY

A planned adult community consisting of two parts: The Fountains, a rental community providing catered and assisted living; and The Kiva, a skilled nursing/health care center. Established in 1978 and built by Gosnell Development. Privately owned and operated by three individuals located in Phoenix and California.

HOUSING TYPES AVAILABLE

Unfurnished and furnished studio, one-bedroom, and two-bedroom apartments available in small two-story clusters of buildings with elevators. All apartments open outward onto covered walkways. Apartments range in size from 400 to over 700 sq ft; six models are available, some with balconies. The apartments are spacious and well designed and include handicapped accessibility. They do not have full kitchens but rather very nice kitchenettes each with small ranges and refrigerators. There is also a 24-hour emergency call system.

NUMBER OF SITES/UNITS

130 apartments at The Fountains.

LOCATION

Scottsdale Village Square is located near central Scottsdale, directly next to a small shopping center. The community is very convenient to everything Scottsdale has to offer. Hospitals, physicians' offices, churches, and shopping are nearby.

REQUIREMENTS/RESTRICTIONS

No minimum age requirement. Pets allowed with some restrictions.

FEES

Studio apartments range from $825 to $850 per month; one bedrooms from $940 to $1075; and two bedrooms from $1265 to $1300 for one person. Furnished apartments are available at a higher charge. There is an additional person charge of $275 to $300 per month. Fees include two meals a day, all utilities, weekly maid services, scheduled transportation, cable TV, and the use of all amenities.

AMENITIES

Scottsdale Village Square amenities include a swimming pool, an attractive dining room, a barber shop and beauty parlor, and organized activity programs. A lot of emphasis is placed on amenities/services to persons needing an assisted living situation (a wide array of services is available but there are additional charges). The village itself is designed in a pleasing manner with courtyards and beautiful landscaping.

REVIEWER'S NOTES

For persons looking for catered and assisted living services, this community offers a lot. You also have the security of a skilled nursing facility owned and operated by the same management. For persons looking for a rental this is an attractive alternative.

THE SPRINGS OF SCOTTSDALE

Rent

3212 North Miller Road
Scottsdale, AZ 85251
(602) 941-9026

INDEPENDENT LIVING FACILITY

A planned rental community for adults. Established in 1987 and owned and operated by Pacific Scene, San Diego; managed by The Springs Management Company. The same group owns and manages two other communities in Mesa, Arizona and four in California.

HOUSING TYPES AVAILABLE

One- and two-bedroom apartments in a three-story elevator building built in a rectangle around central courtyards. All apartments are one level; the one-bedroom units are 750 sq ft; two bedrooms, 1015 sq ft. There are three one-bedroom floor plans to choose from and one two-bedroom plan. The building has an elegant resort-type atmosphere with furnishings and interior design in a southwestern motif. The apartments all open inward to wide corridors—you do not need to go outside to get anywhere in the community. The apartments are spacious, with good closet space, wide doors, and bathrooms with guardrails and walk-in showers. While not specifically catering to the handicapped, accessibility is good.

NUMBER OF SITES/UNITS

138 units.

LOCATION

The Springs is located in central Scottsdale near everything Scottsdale has to offer. You are within minutes of hospitals, doctors, major shopping and recreational facilities, and churches. The "Molly Trolley," a community trolley service to shopping, stops at your door. The Phoenix airport is 15 to 20 minutes away in nonrush-hour traffic.

REQUIREMENTS/RESTRICTIONS

Minimum age 62. Small pets are permitted.

FEES

One-bedroom unfurnished apartments rent for $1350 to $1575 per month; two-bedroom apartments from $1625 to $1800 per month for one person. There is a second person charge of $300. Services included in the monthly rent are two meals a day, weekly housekeeping, scheduled transportation, 24-hour staffing, social activities, covered parking, and all utilities except telephone.

AMENITIES

Apartment amenities in addition to those mentioned earlier include emergency call systems in bedrooms and bathrooms, smoke detector and sprinkler systems, and a private patio or balcony. Community amenities include an elegant dining room (offering restaurant-style dining), a heated swimming pool, a private dining room for resident use, a beauty shop, an ice cream parlor, a billiards room, a library, arts and crafts and game rooms, and scheduled transportation.

REVIEWER'S NOTES

The Springs of Scottsdale is an elegant rental community located in the heart of Scottsdale. For someone who is used to an elegant, catered lifestyle this could be an excellent choice.

VILLA OCOTILLO

Rent

3327 North Civic Center Plaza

Scottsdale, AZ 85251

(602) 946-7111

Opal Paden, Executive Director

INDEPENDENT LIVING FACILITY

A rental community for adults seeking catered or assisted living services. Established in 1970. Owned and operated since November 1988 by Retirement Living Affiliates of Scottsdale, Arizona.

HOUSING TYPES AVAILABLE

Private rooms/studios, one- and two-bedroom units, unfurnished and furnished apartments in a two-story enclosed elevator building. The apartments are available in a variety of models. Studios (private and deluxe private) range from 275 to 375 sq ft, one-bedroom units (suite, mini-suite, and kitchen suite) range from 480 to 650 sq ft. All have balconies or patios. Not all apartments have kitchens—mini-suites and kitchen suites do. All apartments open onto wide hallways and have bathrooms with specially designed tubs or showers with guardrails.

NUMBER OF SITES/UNITS

104 apartments.

LOCATION

Villa Ocotillo is located in the heart of Scottsdale. You are only a few blocks away from Scottsdale Memorial Hospital, shops, a public library, a post office, churches, and recreational activities.

REQUIREMENTS/RESTRICTIONS

No specific age requirement but persons 60 or older preferred. Small pets allowed.

FEES

Monthly rental fees for studio apartments range from $785 to $1055; one bedrooms, $1165 to $1495; two bedrooms, $1550 for one person. There is an additional person charge of $290 per month. Fees include three meals a day, housekeeping, bath and bed linens, 24-hour staffing, all utilities (except telephone), extensive social activities, covered parking, and use of all facilities. The fees also include chauffeured transportation, both scheduled and unscheduled, and a personal shopping service.

AMENITIES

Villa Ocotillo amenities include restaurant-style dining, an outdoor swimming pool, an extensive activities program, games, billiards and cards, a library, a crafts room, and television lounges.

REVIEWER'S NOTES

Villa Ocotillo is an older rental community currently undergoing renovations by its new owners—Retirement Living Affiliates. While neither as new nor as fancy as some competitors, it is comfortable and has charm. The staff seems to be caring and professional.

WESTMINISTER VILLAGE

Buy

12000 North 90th Street

Scottsdale, AZ 85260

(602) 451-2000

INDEPENDENT LIVING FACILITY

A lifecare community established in 1982. Westminister Village is owned by a local nonprofit corporation and managed by Parkside Senior Services, a division of the Lutheran General Hospital System.

HOUSING TYPES AVAILABLE

Studio alcoves and one- and two-bedroom apartments available in two- and three-story enclosed elevator buildings. There are nine models to choose from. The apartments are attractive and provide emergency call systems, guardrails, and walk-in showers in the bathrooms. All apartments open inward and residents can reach any part of the complex without going outside. All apartments have a patio or balcony and kitchens.

NUMBER OF SITES/UNITS

250 apartments with a 60-bed skilled nursing facility.

LOCATION

Westminister Village is located in northeast Scottsdale in a newer part of town. The area surrounding the community is upscale residential. While somewhat removed from central Scottsdale, the Village is still convenient to hospitals (within one mile), physicians' offices, shopping, and recreation. Paradise Valley Mall is about five miles away. The Phoenix airport is 30 to 40 minutes in nonrush-hour traffic.

REQUIREMENTS/RESTRICTIONS

62 or older; pets allowed.

FEES

Entrance fees range from $45,000 (alcove) to $90,250 (two-bedroom unit). The second person entrance fee is $4000. This fee, along with a monthly fee, entitles a person to lifetime residency in the apartment of choice and provision of lifetime nursing center care at the center located at the Village. Monthly service fees start at $800 per person for an alcove; $875 to $1000 for a one-bedroom unit; and $1125 to $1475 for a two bedroom. There is a second person monthly charge of $475. Services included in the monthly fees are one meal a day, 24-hour staffing, scheduled transportation, all utilities (except cable TV and telephone), regular housekeeping, security, social activities, and use of all community amenities. Additional assisted living services are available at no additional charge (you should check further based on your individual needs; other facilities do charge for extra services).

AMENITIES

Westminister Village amenities include a large outdoor swimming pool and Jacuzzi, a general store, gift shop, beauty and barber shop, elegant dining room (restaurant style), private dining room, ice cream parlor, library, exercise rooms, and spacious recreation lounges. There are also church services and a bank on site.

REVIEWER'S NOTES

Westminister Village is a modern, attractive lifecare community. Parkside Senior Services has an excellent reputation, and the people we met seemed very professional. The community itself has a spacious, open feeling that we liked. If you are looking for an elegant community with comprehensive assisted living/medical services, you should visit Westminister.

EL DORADO

Buy

10330 West Thunderbird Boulevard

Sun City, AZ 85351

(602) 972-3000

INDEPENDENT LIVING FACILITY

A full-service planned retirement community. Newly built and managed by HBE Retirement Communities, a division of HBE Corporation.

HOUSING TYPES AVAILABLE

Condominiums with one and two bedrooms (625 to 1450 sq ft). The completed models were well laid out with good closet space and large bathrooms to accommodate wheelchairs. Security call boxes installed in the bathrooms are monitored on a 24-hour basis. All hallways are enclosed and extra wide to accommodate wheelchairs and walkers.

NUMBER OF SITES/UNITS

249 units.

LOCATION

El Dorado is located in the heart of Sun City, right next door to Boswell Hospital. Situated on slightly over seven acres, it is on the south shore of 27-acre Viewpoint Lake. All necessary services and conveniences are within five miles. Banks, churches, malls, and medical offices are within one mile. Phoenix airport is approximately 30 miles away.

REQUIREMENTS/RESTRICTIONS

Minimum age 55 for all residents. Visiting privileges for children. No pets.

FEES

El Dorado condominium prices begin at $69,900 for one bedroom with 625 sq ft; larger, 850-sq-ft one-bedroom models are $123,900. The two-bedroom models, 950 and 1450 sq ft, are $109,900 and $199,900, respectively. Monthly service fees range from $500 to $750, depending on the size of the unit purchased. The monthly fee includes one weekly linen service, building and grounds maintenance, regularly scheduled transportation, 24-hour staffed security, emergency call system with intercom, and fire sprinkler system throughout.

AMENITIES

In addition to the services and amenities covered by the monthly fee, El Dorado offers: a swimming pool, lakeview golf course, fishing in the adjacent lake, a library, arts and crafts rooms, a fitness program, and scheduled trips and activities. As a homeowner you are entitled to full membership privileges at Sun City Recreational Center Inc. The "Care for Life" program provides support services designed to keep you independent and in your own home. (This is not a lifecare facility, and all units sold are deeded to you). A staff nurse and other health care workers work to keep you healthy (included in monthly fee) and will work with you to coordinate any services required from more specifically trained medical personnel.

REVIEWER'S NOTES

El Dorado provides a resort-style setting for those desiring an alternative to lifecare facilities and outright ownership of their homes. Residents wishing the security and comfort of staff medical personnel will appreciate El Dorado. The central location and the decorator apartments will also appeal to those who are active and enjoy a resort-style residence. The staff with whom we came in contact appeared honest and reliable.

ROYAL OAKS

Buy

10015 Royal Oak Road
Sun City, AZ
85351
(602) 933-2807

INDEPENDENT LIVING FACILITY

A lifecare community in the heart of Sun City. Owned and operated by People of Faith, Inc.

HOUSING TYPES AVAILABLE

Apartments are offered with six different floor plans. The alcove (studio) unit has 504 sq ft and includes a small kitchen, walk-in closet, and a balcony with an enclosed storage closet. The two one-bedroom, one-bath models have either 649 or 792 sq ft. Both have kitchens, small dining alcoves, living rooms, and balconies with storage. There are three two-bedroom, two-bath models ranging from 986 to 1456 sq ft; the two largest have laundry rooms. The apartment complex is three story with interior hallways. Garden homes (duplexes) are offered in ten different floor plans. These homes are all single story and have covered patios and garages. Three one-bedroom, one-bath units range in size from 838 to 916 sq ft. All seven two-bedroom units have two baths and range between 1040 and 1660 sq ft. The largest has a breakfast room that leads to the covered patio as well as a separate Arizona room (den). Both the apartments and duplexes are designed to maximize available living space.

NUMBER OF SITES/UNITS

249 apartments, 100 duplexes, and a 100-bed nursing center.

LOCATION

Royal Oaks occupies 32 acres within Sun City. All services, medical facilities, shopping, churches, and recreation are well within a five-mile radius.

REQUIREMENTS/RESTRICTIONS

Minimum age 62. No pets.

FEES

The entrance fee for a studio apartment is $36,000 (only a single occupant allowed). One-bedroom apartments are $45,000 and $54,000. The two-bedroom apartments run $67,000, $79,500, and $96,000. Prices listed are for a single occupant. A second person is $4000 for all units. Entrance fees for one-bedroom duplex models range from $61,600 to $65,700. The seven two-bedroom duplexes range from $74,200 to $116,600. The additional cost for a second person is $4000. Monthly service fees are based on unit size. Apartments run between $657 and $1252 monthly, with $407 additional for a second person. Duplexes range from $845 to $1346 ($407 more for a second person). Services included in the monthly fees are one meal daily in the elegant dining room, all utilities (except telephone), scheduled transportation, an emergency call system in each unit, planned activities, use of common areas, biweekly housekeeping, weekly linen service, and building and grounds maintenance. Basic and skilled nursing care covered by the service fee provides a semiprivate room for an unlimited period of time. Each resident admitted is responsible for the payment of personal physicians, private nurses, medicine, physical therapy, and other "extras." Medicare and supplemental insurance will be paid to the facility. Entrance fees are refundable only after the facility has deducted 10 percent of the initial fee and 1 percent for each month of residency. After seven-and-one-half years of residency no refunds will be made. In cases of death, no refunds are given. If there is a resident survivor, that person can continue to reside in the same apartment.

AMENITIES

Recreational facilities, including a heated pool, are available to residents and their guests in addition to the amenities listed in the fees section. Residents may elect to pay $100 per person for the Sun City Recreation Centers privilege card. The card allows full use of all Sun City Recreation Centers facilities.

REVIEWER'S NOTES

Royal Oaks is a large and attractive facility. The duplexes have sizable desert-landscaped yards around them and are not crowded into a small area. The apartment complex is in a wagon-wheel formation in the center of the facility. The separation of independent living sections and nursing facilities gives the impression of two distinct communities. Persons desiring a Sun City location and the reassurance of lifecare should contact this facility for more information.

Lake Powell Resorts & Marinas/ARA Leisure Services.

RYERSON HERITAGE

17404 North 99th Avenue

Sun City, AZ 85373

(602) 977-2777

Buy

INDEPENDENT LIVING FACILITY

A luxury condominium community in Sun City. Established less than five years ago and owned by the Ryerson Company.

HOUSING TYPES AVAILABLE

Condominiums offered in four floor plans. The facility comprises three stories and is built around a central courtyard. Model A is a one-bedroom, one-bath unit with 851 sq ft. Models B, C, and D have two bedrooms and two baths and 1110, 1296, and 1427 sq ft, respectively. Units have either a patio or balcony with an enclosed storage/laundry room.

NUMBER OF SITES/UNITS

100 units.

LOCATION

The Ryerson Heritage is located in the heart of Sun City and offers residents a central and convenient location. All services and health care facilities are located well within a five-mile radius. Recreation facilities and golf courses belonging to Del Webb's Sun City are available to residents for a moderate fee (usually negotiated by Heritage management annually).

REQUIREMENTS/RESTRICTIONS

Minimum age 55 (one household member). Pets under 18 inches permitted but with strict containment rules.

FEES

Prices for new condominiums with one bedroom, one bath (model A) range from $64,730 to $74,750 depending on the floor. The two-bedroom, two-bath models range from $97,300 to $125,100. Resales are handled by the on-site sales office. The homeowners' association fee, assessed monthly, is currently $185.

AMENITIES

Available amenities include a pool and spa, recreation rooms and lounge, covered parking, outside maintenance, and a full-time resident manager. Security begins at the locked front door with a call box/intercom. Individual units have emergency call boxes. There are lounges and/or game rooms on every floor.

REVIEWER'S NOTES

Although Ryerson Heritage is somewhat more expensive than similar facilities in the same area, it will appeal to persons desiring secure and elegant condominium living. The units are well designed for gracious living. The well-appointed common areas can be made available to residents for private parties. The atmosphere reminded us of the luxury apartments on the East Coast.

SUN CITY

Buy

West Bell Road

Sun City, AZ 85351

INDEPENDENT LIVING FACILITY

A master-planned adult community city. The largest "adults only" community in the country and the prototype for the active retirement community. Begun in 1960 by Del Webb, it was sold out by the mid-1970s.

HOUSING TYPES AVAILABLE

Single-family homes, the majority having two bedrooms and two baths and ranging in size from 1100 to 2000 sq ft. There are a fair number of three-bedroom homes with more square footage, as well as duplexes—mostly two bedroom, two bath with about 1600 sq ft. Several condominium complexes exist with a variety of floor plans.

NUMBER OF SITES/UNITS

Over 46,000 residents.

LOCATION

Sun City is located to the north and west of Phoenix, about 30 miles from the downtown area. It is a self-contained community with all services and conveniences (except an airport) located within its confines. There are two hospitals, special clinics, and physicians in all specialties. Sun City is characterized by wide streets, many golf courses, and well-kept homes. Transportation is by car or golf cart. There is Dial-a-Ride service available to those not wishing to drive; the fares within Sun City are moderate.

REQUIREMENTS/RESTRICTIONS

Minimum age is 50 for at least one member of the household. No children as permanent residents.

FEES

All residences for sale are preowned. Prices vary with the market. A good selection of homes is almost always available. Those listed here are taken from a sample of homes on the market in July 1989. Single family homes (two bedroom, two bath) began at $45,900 and went up to $290,000. Duplexes were offered from $49,900 and the condos then on the market were in the $100,000-plus range. Homeowner fees vary by type. Single family homeowners pay a one-time fee of $300 and then $100 per person per year. This gives you access to all recreation and golf facilities.

AMENITIES

Eleven golf courses, three of which are private, are available. There are seven recreation centers around Sun City—one for each neighborhood—and all are accessible to residents. There are pools and parks, and each neighborhood has its own individual character. Twenty-six religions are represented in the area. Sun City has the lowest crime rate in the country.

REVIEWER'S NOTES

Sun City is on such a large scale that it is impossible to describe in a few words. It is appealing to those desiring a large community devoted to active adults. There are so many facilities and activities available that one should plan to spend at least an afternoon exploring the community. There are hotels and RV parks in the area and vacation packages are available through Del Webb. For more information about visiting, call (800) 528-2604 or in Arizona (602) 975-2270, extension 3057.

WOODDALE VILLAGE

Rent

18616 North 99th Avenue
Sun City, AZ 85373
(602) 933-1313

INDEPENDENT LIVING FACILITY

A facility incorporating independent living apartments, a catered living section, and a care facility. Established in 1984 and continuously owned by the Lutheran Brethren.

HOUSING TYPES AVAILABLE

Apartments in two-story elevator buildings. All apartments have front and back doors that open to covered outdoor hallways. The studio apartment is 527 sq ft and has both a small bedroom and a kitchen separate from the living room. Two one-bedroom, one-bath models range from 793 to 873 sq ft. There are also two models of the two-bedroom, two-bath apartments that have either 1008 or 1118 sq ft. All apartments have back patios with enclosed storage closets.

NUMBER OF SITES/UNITS

155 apartments, including both independent and catered living; a 100-bed care center.

LOCATION

Wooddale is surrounded by Sun City and shares the same broad range of commercial and medical services.

REQUIREMENTS/RESTRICTIONS

Minimum age 50. Pets under 15 pounds allowed.

FEES

Monthly rent for independent living for one person starts at $685 (studio) and goes up to $1169 (large two bedroom). Two-person occupancy ranges from $745 to $1229. This includes breakfast, local transportation, a 24-hour emergency call system in apartments, the use of the pool, and organized social activities. Catered living apartments (with the same floor plans) range from $1600 to $1820 for singles and from $2200 to $2500 for couples. In addition to the services listed above, this includes three meals daily, a nurse on 24-hour call, weekly housekeeping, and flat laundry service (linens). Additional meals for residents are $75 for lunch, $150 for dinner, or both for $215 monthly. Meals can be purchased on a per-day basis. Sun City facilities are available to Wooddale Village residents upon obtaining a "privilege card." It should be mentioned that residents accrue a maximum of 12 credit days per year for use in the Wooddale Health Care Center. Residents begin to accrue days after 90 days of occupancy (6 days).

AMENITIES

Resident transportation is provided by a 24-passenger bus that makes scheduled trips to shopping, banking, and social activities. Two cars are available to take residents to medical appointments. Guest apartments are available for family and friends. A beauty/barber shop is on site, as well as storage space for golf carts. The location itself should be considered as an amenity in this case.

REVIEWER'S NOTES

Wooddale Village seems to have a caring staff (some of whom are also residents) and a comfortable unpretentious feeling to it. It was nice to find a studio apartment with a separate bedroom and kitchen that could accommodate two persons. This facility might be a good choice for those wishing to rent but still have access to Sun City facilities (golf courses and recreation centers).

MADISON HOUSE/SUN CITY WEST

Rent

18626 Spanish
Garden Drive
Sun City West,
AZ 85375
(602) 584-1999

INDEPENDENT LIVING FACILITY

A planned apartment rental community for mature adults desiring catered or assisted living amenities. Established in March 1986 and developed, owned, and managed by Camorco/Madison House, a subsidiary of the Danmor Corporation of Bellevue, Washington, which operates two similar communities in Oregon and Washington.

HOUSING TYPES AVAILABLE

One- and two-bedroom apartments available in a three-story complex. One-bedroom apartments have over 600 sq ft; and two-bedroom apartments are over 900. All units are single level with decks and sprinkler and fire alarm systems. Apartments are attractive and have a nice open feeling. The Tower Club consists of 63 apartments offering more extensive assisted living services.

NUMBER OF SITES/UNITS

196 units including 63 Tower Club apartments.

LOCATION

Madison House is located in the heart of Sun City West, one of the largest retirement developments in the Southwest. Every imaginable activity and amenity is available in this retirement area, which has invested over $70 million in amenities. As a resident of Madison House, you are eligible for membership in Sun City West recreation clubs—a major plus if you are interested in activities. Sun City West is located to the north and west of Phoenix and its earlier sister development of Sun City. It is approximately 40 miles from the downtown Phoenix area. There are two hospitals, special clinics, and physicians in all specialities.

REQUIREMENTS/RESTRICTIONS

Minimum age 55. Small pets are permitted in first-floor apartments.

FEES

One-bedroom apartments rent from $1695 to $1995 per month; two bedrooms from $2195 to $2795. There is a $200 per month additional person charge. These fees include three meals a day, all utilities, weekly maid service, chauffeured transportation, 24-hour staff, use of all amenities and services, and fully paid membership in Sun City West recreation centers. Madison House also rents to winter visitors if apartments are available. For specific rates please call (602) 584-1999.

AMENITIES

Madison House is an elegant rental community with extensive services and amenities. There is a swimming pool, fitness center, social director to plan tours, trips and events, an RN on staff, and rooms for clubs and activities. The complex is laid out in a very attractive fashion with entrance from a lobby with a reception desk. Dining is either inside in the attractive Madison Room or outside on the terrace.

REVIEWER'S NOTES

This is an attractive planned community for people looking to rent or no longer wishing to maintain a home, and desiring catered or assisted living services. It is appropriate for active, completely independent people as well as those who are still independent but need some medical or personal assistance. The development is elegant and comfortable and the location very convenient.

SUN CITY WEST

Buy

13323 Meeker Boulevard

Sun City West, AZ 85372

(602) 975-2270; (800) 341-6121

INDEPENDENT LIVING FACILITY

A master-planned active retirement community. Founded in 1978 by the Del Webb Corporation.

HOUSING TYPES AVAILABLE

Single-family homes from 1000 sq ft to more than 2800 sq ft. Duplexes ranging in size from 933 to 1882 sq ft. Executive villas have either 1425 or 1975 sq ft. There are 21 models (open to the public) to choose from at the new homes sales center. Preowned homes are listed through local realty agencies.

NUMBER OF SITES/UNITS

Currently 18,500 residents. New home sites should be available through 1994.

LOCATION

Sun City West lies two miles west of the original Sun City. The two areas provide all types of businesses and services. The Del Webb Hospital is located in Sun City West, along with physicians' offices and special clinics. All major religious denominations hold services within five miles. Lake Pleasant recreational area is less than 30 minutes away by car. The Phoenix airport is a 45-minute drive during off-peak hours.

REQUIREMENTS/RESTRICTIONS

Minimum age 55 for one resident in the household.

FEES

New single-family homes with two bedrooms and two baths begin at $68,500 (1038 sq ft) and climb to $194,900 for the largest model (2790 sq ft), which has two-bedroom suites, two baths, a den (an optional third bedroom), and Arizona room. New duplexes—all two bedroom, two bath—start at $79,900 (1165 sq ft) and go up to $118,900 (1880 sq ft). Executive Villas available in two floor plans—both with two bedrooms and two baths—are priced at $113,000 (1425 sq ft) and $133,600 (1975 sq ft). The greens fee for residents who golf is $13. Existing homes are sometimes available for lease for long or short terms. Units vary in price depending on season, furnishings, and home size. Unfurnished units on a long-term lease may range from $400 to $1000 per month. Contact the rental department at (602) 975-3077.

AMENITIES

Every imaginable activity is available in Sun City West. Over $70 million has been spent on amenities. Here is a partial listing: Sundome Performing Arts Center, 14-million-dollar R. H. Johnson Recreation Center, five golf courses, a country club with a private golf course and two additional 5-million-dollar park and recreation centers, and security patrols staffed by volunteers.

REVIEWER'S NOTES

It is difficult not to be impressed by Sun City West. It may not be to your individual liking, but if you are in the Phoenix area it should be seen. The houses are very open and light, with the relaxed southwestern lifestyle in mind. The largest duplex and the smallest and largest single family homes were especially attractive. The executive villas are reported to be very popular. Sun City West has vacation packages that allow you to sample the lifestyle. Call (800) 528-2604 for more information.

SUN LAKES

25612 E.J. Robson Boulevard

Sun Lakes, AZ 85248

(602) 895-9600

Buy

INDEPENDENT LIVING FACILITY

One of the earliest and most popular active adult communities in Arizona. Developed by E.J. Robson, who is also the developer of Saddlebrooke in Tucson.

HOUSING TYPES AVAILABLE

Single-family homes, two and three bedroom, with 14 models and several different roof elevations to choose from. Square footage ranges from 1361 to 2914 depending on the model. The homes are all single level, with mission tile roofs, cathedral ceilings, and open kitchens and dining rooms. Resales are available.

NUMBER OF SITES/UNITS

Currently over 8000 residents.

LOCATION

Sun Lakes is located 25 miles south of Phoenix just off Interstate Highway 10. Despite the growth of Phoenix and Chandler (just to the north), Sun Lakes remains private and isolated from the urban rush. The growth of Chandler has actually brought certain services closer to Sun Lakes. The Phoenix airport is about 25 minutes away in off-peak hours.

REQUIREMENTS/RESTRICTIONS

Developed for adults 40 and over.

FEES

New single-family homes start at $89,695 for a two bedroom, two bath and climb to over $200,000 depending on the model and lot chosen. Homeowners fees are $37.50 per month per household of two people for all recreational facilities (except golf), maintenance of common areas, fire protection, and security. Golf fees are either a daily green fee of $14-$20 depending on the season or an annual membership fee per person ranging from $425 to $850 depending on course selected. Sun Lakes has an innovative lot purchase plan for people interested in advance purchases. The plan allows you to purchase your lot and take up to two years to begin construction of your home.

AMENITIES

Sun Lakes amenities are extensive and need to be seen to be appreciated. All types of services and amenities are available in the immediate area. Recreational facilities revolve around three country clubs, a $10 million recreational facility, three golf courses, swimming pools, tennis courts, health spas, and an arts and crafts center.

REVIEWER'S NOTES

Sun Lakes is one of the first and most successful of the active adult communities in Arizona. It caters to a somewhat younger group who enjoy recreational amenities. E.J. Robson has a style that is characteristic of this community and Saddlebrooke in Tucson. His houses are open and spacious, and the community amenities are extensive.

HAPPY TRAILS RESORTS

17200 West Bell Road

Surprise, AZ 85374-9740

(602) 975-5040; (800) 872-4579

First United Realty, Inc.

INDEPENDENT LIVING FACILITY

A mobile home and RV resort with a golf course, located on 320 acres. A property of Western Savings.

HOUSING TYPES AVAILABLE

Mobile homes for sale in a variety of sizes and price ranges. Vacation Villas (mobile homes) are landscaped and completely furnished with either one or two bedrooms. The one-bedroom model is 14 by 36 ft (504 sq ft); and the two bedroom is 14 by 44 ft (616 sq ft). RV lots for sale or rent are 2500 to 6000 sq ft and have complete hookups.

NUMBER OF SITES/UNITS

No information on the total number of sites.

LOCATION

Surprise, AZ is 50 minutes away from downtown Phoenix. Happy Trails is a large resort surrounded by plenty of wide open space. Sun City medical facilities and shopping are a 10-minute drive. Lake Pleasant is less than 30 minutes away.

REQUIREMENTS/RESTRICTIONS

Minimum age 55. Pets are permitted.

FEES

The vacation villas (lot included) range from $38,000 to $53,000. New park model mobile homes start at $13,900, which includes delivery and setup. Lots start at around $20,000. RV lots can be purchased for $21,900 to $41,800. The monthly rental rate for RV lots is $340 and includes water, electric, sewer, cable TV, and telephone. Call for rental rates for the vacation villas. Golf course fees are $8.00 for nine holes and $12.75 for 18. Yearly memberships can be purchased for $375 (single) or $625 (couple). Association dues, for which owners are assessed on a monthly basis, run between $60 and $75 depending on the unit. The dues cover water, garbage, sewers, and cable TV.

AMENITIES

The nine-hole golf course (soon to be 18) was designed by Ken Kavanaugh and is a par 36. The main recreation center is 48,000 sq ft and includes a post office, general store, ballroom, TV and game rooms, a cafeteria, and Roy Rogers and Dale Evans gallery. There are also neighborhood centers each with laundry facilities and a swimming pool. The community has four swimming pools, six tennis courts, 12 billiard tables, and a fitness center with exercise equipment.

REVIEWER'S NOTES

Happy Trails features Roy Rogers and Dale Evans as spokespersons but the community bears little resemblance to the "old west." The community is very large and seems to be in excellent condition throughout. Even during an August visit there was a lot of activity to be seen—109 degrees notwithstanding. Although the location may seem remote, it is still only minutes away from Sun City West. Winter visitors should make reservations well in advance as this spot is very popular.

SUN VILLAGE

Buy

14300 West Bell
Road
Surprise, AZ
85374
(602) 271-4242;
(800) 654-9969

INDEPENDENT LIVING FACILITY

A master-planned adult community in a rural setting 1 mile west of Sun City West. Established in 1986, owned and managed by the Radnor Corporation, a real estate subsidiary of the Sun Company, Inc.

HOUSING TYPES AVAILABLE

Single-family homes, garden homes (detached), and resort villas (condominiums). Each of the three major housing types is built on one floor and is architecturally distinct. Resort villas are offered in four floor plans ranging from 620 to 908 sq ft. The two smaller models have one bath and the two larger have two baths. These homes may be ideal for those people looking for a second or winter home. Garden villas are offered in eight floor plans. These range in square footage from 1027 to 1478. Designed to allow the second or third bedroom to be used as a den, these models all have a light, open feel. The ceilings are vaulted and there are many interesting and unusual design features. The single-family homes are available in seven, exceptionally attractive floor plans. Ranging in size from 1250 to 1995 sq ft, these homes are all designed to maximize living space and facilitate entertaining.

NUMBER OF SITES/UNITS

1800 to 2000 residents when sold out. Currently about 400 homes have been sold.

LOCATION

Sun Village is located in Surprise, Arizona (a rural farming community). The area adjacent to the facility is undeveloped for several miles on all but one side. There is a new housing development to the north. Sun City West, which is only 5 minutes away, offers an abundance of medical services, shopping, entertainment, and churches. This community is rural in feeling while being convenient to important services. Downtown Phoenix is approximately 35 miles away.

REQUIREMENTS/RESTRICTIONS

Adults only. The plan is to have 80 percent of residents over age 55 and 20 percent between 40 and 55 when the community is complete. Pets are permitted.

FEES

Resort villas are priced from $46,400 to $60,300. Garden homes range from $71,800 to $90,700, while the single-family homes sell for $78,900 to $110,900. All prices listed are for standard features; upgraded features are extra. Information on homeowners' fees vary by product type.

AMENITIES

There is a security gate at the entrance, staffed 24 hours a day. Recreational features are a nine-hole golf course with a pro shop, one of Arizona's largest heated swimming pools, tennis courts, a large recreation/community center with rooms for all types of social or artistic pursuits as well as a restaurant. Homes are wired for security and many options are available to customize the model you select. An RV storage lot is available within the community.

REVIEWER'S NOTES

Sun Village offers the most attractive and unique models that I have seen in the Southwest. The accessibility to the Sun Cities should not be overlooked. For some reason, this community is as yet "undiscovered." I would suggest a visit, as it may be exactly what you are looking for.

SUNFLOWER RESORT

16501 El Mirage Road

Surprise, AZ 85374-3601

(800) 627-8637; (602) 583-0100

INDEPENDENT LIVING FACILITY

An adults-only recreational vehicle community, owned by a subsidiary of National Mobile Development Co.

HOUSING TYPES AVAILABLE

Spaces for your RV with full electrical hookups, water, and sewer.

NUMBER OF SITES/UNITS

1107 spaces.

LOCATION

Surprise is northwest of Phoenix. Its neighbors are Sun City and Peoria. The population of the area is primarily composed of retirees, and because of its proximity to Sun City, local businesses and services cater to this segment of the population. Within a five-mile radius are two hospitals, many physicians, and shopping, and services are held for most major religious denominations. Surprise is about 30 miles from downtown Phoenix.

REQUIREMENTS/RESTRICTIONS

Adults 40 years or older. Deposits due on advance reservations.

FEES

Daily rates are $18; weekly, $108. Both daily and weekly rates include electricity. The monthly rate is $325 and yearly rates range from $1375 to $1625 (depending on location); you are responsible for your electric bill on monthly and yearly rates. These rates are based on occupancy by two people. There is an additional charge for an extra person based on length of stay.

AMENITIES

There is a staffed security station at the entrance to the park. Refuse collection, sewer, water, mail boxes, and fire protection are provided to all residents. Sunflower has a large Spanish-style recreation center that is for the use of its residents. Activities and facilities include card rooms, an olympic-size swimming pool, a Jacuzzi, billiards, dances, movies, crafts classes, and tennis. There are laundry facilities on site. You are within walking distance of a supermarket and restaurant.

REVIEWER'S NOTES

Sunflower Resort is located in one of Arizona's most popular retirement areas. This park is very popular with all types of RV owners, and residents seem to like the community atmosphere in the clubhouse. The security check-in at the entrance was reassuringly thorough.

FRIENDSHIP VILLAGE OF TEMPE

Buy

2645 East
Southern Avenue
Tempe, AZ
85282
(602) 831-5000;
(800) 824-1112

INDEPENDENT LIVING FACILITY

A lifecare community established in 1980 and owned and operated by a not-for-profit community board.

HOUSING TYPES AVAILABLE

Studio, alcove, one-, two-, and three-bedroom apartments available in three-story elevator buildings; one- and two-bedroom garden homes available in duplexes and fourplexes. Garden homes are spacious with full kitchens. Bathrooms are good sized and provide grab bars in the bath and shower; emergency call cords have been installed in each bedroom and bath. One-bedroom homes range from 675 to 840 sq ft; two bedrooms, 950 to 1538 sq ft. All have covered patios and covered parking. Apartments range from 308 sq ft (studio); 440 sq ft (alcove); 576 to 748 sq ft (one bedroom); 792 to 1060 sq ft (two bedroom); to 1152 sq ft (three bedroom). All apartments have kitchens, good-sized bathrooms, handicapped accessibility, wide doors, and emergency call systems. All apartments open inward to wide hallways.

NUMBER OF SITES/UNITS

212 apartments and 297 garden homes on 46 acres with a 120-bed skilled nursing facility.

LOCATION

Friendship Village is located in east Tempe just north of Superstition Freeway on Southern Avenue. The location is excellent in terms of convenience to services in the Tempe and Mesa areas and accessibility to the Phoenix airport. There is a major hospital right next door to the community, and Fiesta Mall is only a short distance away.

REQUIREMENTS/RESTRICTIONS

62 or older; spouse can be 55 but is not covered under lifecare until 62. Cats allowed in garden homes; no dogs.

FEES

Entrance fees for apartments under the Standard Plan are $33,750 for a studio, $45,850 for an alcove, $56,000 to $70,250 for a one bedroom, $73,750 to $90,900 for a two bedroom, and $99,900 for a three bedroom. Entrance fees for garden homes under the standard plan are $64,500 to $74,250 for one-bedroom units, $89,750 to $140,900 for the two bedrooms. In addition to the standard plan, there is a "return of capital" plan under which 90 percent of the entrance fee is refundable given certain conditions. Monthly fees for apartments are $724 for a studio, $808 for an alcove, $889 to $938 for one-bedroom units, $972 to $1069 for two-bedroom units, and $1139 for the three-bedroom model. There is an additional person charge of $446 per month. Garden home monthly fees are $972 to $1021, one bedroom; $1047 to $1529, two bedroom. The additional person charge is $473. These fees include one meal daily, all utilities, housekeeping twice a month, weekly flat laundry, maintenance of grounds, security, 24-hour staffing, scheduled transportation, and use of all community facilities and services. Health services include unlimited use of the on-site skilled nursing facility. The only additional charge is for two meals.

AMENITIES

Friendship Village offers a very impressive range of amenities including an attractive dining room, large convocation hall, library, billiards room, lounges, clubs and gift shops, the Friendship Center (a 9000-sq-ft activity center), a swimming pool and Jacuzzi, shuffleboard courts, a beauty/barber shop, and on-site banking. It also stresses assisted living services (in-home) provided by full-time home health aides and nurses and the 120-bed Health Care Center.

REVIEWER'S NOTES

This is a beautiful lifecare community with a vast array of services and amenities. Be prepared to stay awhile and take a complete tour. The garden homes provide the feeling of a residential community. If you are looking for an attractive community with assisted living services you should definitely visit Friendship Village.

Prime times at Friendship Village.

What's life-care retirement like at Friendship Village of Tempe?

You'll find the answer on the friendly faces of the residents shown here. Just like hundreds of others over the past 10 years, they're having the times of their lives enjoying Friendship Village's prime lifestyle.

Friendship Village offers an active, independent retirement made secure by the availability of unlimited long-term nursing care. All of this is available in one affordable, predictable financial package, including our Return of Capital™ Plan which protects you or your estate.

When you're ready for prime times, Friendship Village of Tempe is ready to supply them. Just call toll-free for more information: **(800) 824-1112** outside Arizona; **(800) 824-2225** within Arizona; **(602) 831-5000** locally. Or return the coupon.

PRIME·TIMES
10
YEAR
ANNIVERSARY
1980   1990
FRIENDSHIP VILLAGE
OF TEMPE

Please send me more information about life-care retirement at Friendship Village of Tempe, where entrance fees range from $33,750-$149,850. I understand there is no obligation.

Name_____

Address_____

City/State/Zip_____

Telephone_____ Age_____

Single_____ Married_____ Widowed_____

12951

Mail to: Friendship Village of Tempe, 2645 E. Southern Ave., Tempe, AZ 85282
A not-for-profit community.
✿ Managed by Life Care Services Corporation

WESTCHESTER VILLA

Rent

6150 South Rural Road
Tempe, AZ 85283
(602) 897-9130

INDEPENDENT LIVING FACILITY

Westchester Villa in Tempe is in the southeastern area of metropolitan Phoenix. We visited this facility but were not able to see individual apartments. Information was taken from the facility's marketing material. Affiliated with the Volunteers of America Group, the facility is approximately 10 years old.

HOUSING TYPES AVAILABLE

Five apartment models, ranging from studios (430 sq ft) to two bedroom, two bath (1060 sq ft), are available. Apartments are housed in separate clusters of three to six. All clusters are two story with motel-style exterior stairways and hallways (no elevators). There is also a health care facility on site.

NUMBER OF SITES/UNITS

114 apartments.

LOCATION

Westchester Villa is in the south central part of Tempe. Well within a five-mile radius are a large hospital (Desert Samaritan), shopping malls, churches, and Arizona State University. The nearby Superstition Freeway puts travel time to the airport and downtown Phoenix only 15 minutes away. The Mesa area can also be quickly reached. The surrounding neighborhood is mainly residential apartments.

REQUIREMENTS/RESTRICTIONS

Minimum age 55. Call for pet policy.

FEES

Monthly rates we saw began at $575 for the studio; $735 to $795 for one-bedroom models; and $935 to $1075 for the two bedroom. All utilities are included as are weekly housekeeping and scheduled transportation. Meals and additional services are available for an extra charge. Short-term leases may be available in addition to the standard one-year lease.

AMENITIES

Recreational activities include a variety of scheduled events and classes. Outdoor pool and spa, and shuffleboard courts, as well as indoor lounges and rooms for arts and crafts provide residents with places to socialize and exercise. Apartments have emergency call boxes that are monitored around the clock.

REVIEWER'S NOTES

We were disappointed that the staff at Westchester Villa had no time to show us around or answer our questions. While the exterior appeared to be well maintained, it seemed a bit "sterile" to us. The next-door care facility is said to offer care at several levels including supervisory and skilled nursing. Residents in the independent Westchester Villa apartments may receive priority placement at the care center. Our recommendations for this facility can be given only on the basis of price and location. In these two categories Westchester Villa would seem to have average marks.

BROADWAY PROPER

Rent

400 South Broadway Place

Tucson, AZ 85710-3788

(602) 296-3238

INDEPENDENT LIVING FACILITY

A planned apartment rental community for mature adults desiring catered or assisted living amenities. Established in December 1987 and developed, owned, and managed by Decker Company, a local Tucson family.

HOUSING TYPES AVAILABLE

One-, two-, and three-bedroom apartments located in a three-story, all-enclosed elevator building with a central courtyard. Apartments are on one level. One-bedroom apartments range from 403 to 580 sq ft; two bedrooms, from 642 to 801 sq ft; three bedrooms are 912 sq ft. There are 11 floor plans to choose from. The entrance is very attractive and provides a large reception area and lounge. The apartments are spacious with high ceilings.

NUMBER OF SITES/UNITS

232 apartments; 260 additional planned.

LOCATION

Broadway Proper is located in southeast Tucson on Broadway, a major Tucson east-west street. The facility is significantly set back from the street, however, which makes the location more private. It is also adjacent to the Hilton Hotel. The area is well developed and very convenient to shopping, churches, and hospitals.

REQUIREMENTS/RESTRICTIONS

Minimum age 62 (spouse can be younger); pets allowed.

FEES

Small one-bedroom apartments range from $530 per month to $840; two bedrooms range from $795 to $945; three bedrooms, $1055. There is an additional person charge of $200 per month. Services included in the monthly fees are utilities, biweekly maid service, scheduled transportation, activities, and community services. Meals are offered separately: two meals a day for $300 a month; one meal, $200. Continental breakfast is served free of charge to residents who are on a meal plan. Cable TV and telephone are extra.

AMENITIES

Apartments are attractive with high ceilings. Accessibility for the disabled is very good. Extensive community amenities include swimming, activity rooms (Pima Community College holds classes here), library, lounge areas, and a very attractive dining room located on the third floor. There is also a doctor on the premises.

REVIEWER'S NOTES

Broadway Proper is an elegant, comfortable community that we felt had very attractive surroundings without an overwhelming "resort" feeling. There was a lot of activity the day we visited. This seemed to be an active community with a group of residents from 70 to 80 years old.

CAMLU RETIREMENT APARTMENTS

Rent

102 South Sherwood Village Drive

Tucson, AZ 85710

(602) 298-9242

INDEPENDENT LIVING FACILITY

A planned apartment rental community for mature adults desiring assisted living amenities. Established in 1979 and owned and operated by Camlu Corporation, which operates 11 similar facilities throughout the Southwest.

HOUSING TYPES AVAILABLE

Studio and one-bedroom apartments in a two- to three-story apartment complex. One-bedroom apartments are approximately 485 sq ft; studios, about 358. An attractive entrance opens to a lobby, reception desk, and a large general room with a pleasant feeling. The corridors are wide. Since staff was not available to show the housing we cannot comment on the interiors of the apartments.

NUMBER OF SITES/UNITS

160 residents; over 100 units.

LOCATION

Camlu is located on a quiet residential street in a middle class area in southeast Tucson. The location is very convenient to shopping, churches, and hospitals. This area is continuing to develop.

REQUIREMENTS/RESTRICTIONS

Minimum age 62; no pets allowed.

FEES

One-bedroom unfurnished apartments, $780 to $830 per month; studio apartments, $660. There is a second person charge of $250 per month. Services included in the monthly rent are three meals a day, all utilities, weekly housekeeping, scheduled transportation, 24-hour staffing, and social activities. Telephone and cable TV are extra.

AMENITIES

No description is provided on apartment amenities because they were not seen. Camlu offers a "Supervisory Care Wing," which provides additional assisted living services, including assistance with bathing, for fees about 40 to 50 percent higher than those quoted above. Other amenities include a library, an exercise room, and a beauty shop. There is no swimming pool.

REVIEWER'S NOTES

Camlu is located in a convenient part of southeast Tucson, and the community seems pleasant. Most residents appear to be in their 70s or early 80s.

CAMPANA DEL RIO

Rent

1550 East River Road

Tucson, AZ 85718

(602) 299-1941

INDEPENDENT LIVING FACILITY

A planned apartment rental community for mature adults desiring catered or assisted living amenities. Established in March of 1988 by Brim Corporation, the community is now owned and operated by Hillhaven Corporation.

HOUSING TYPES AVAILABLE

Studio, one-bedroom, two-bedroom apartments, and villas are available. Apartments are located in a three-story rectangular complex with a swimming pool in the outdoor central area. Apartments are one level, and studios range in size from 430 to 515 sq ft; one-bedroom apartments, 540 to 592 sq ft; two bedrooms, 658 to 796 sq ft. Villas—all two bedroom with one or two baths—range from 792 to 1015 sq ft. There are 11 floor plans to choose from. The main complex and villas have an elegant resort-type feeling to them. The apartments are spacious with high ceilings. Bathrooms have walk-in showers. There are wide halls but no guardrails.

NUMBER OF SITES/UNITS

191 apartments (24 units for assisted living); 23 villas.

LOCATION

Campana del Rio is located in north Tucson in the scenic and convenient foothills areas. Excellent shopping, recreation, hospitals, and other facilities are within a few minutes. The nearby area can be congested but a car is not necessary due to the transportation amenities provided.

REQUIREMENTS/RESTRICTIONS

Minimum age 55 and over (for couples both must be at least 55); pets under 30 pounds are allowed.

FEES

Studio apartments rent for $795 to $895 per month; one bedroom, $925 to $1050; two bedroom, $1095 to $1300; and villas, $1300 to $1500. There is a second person charge of $250. Services covered by the monthly fee include two meals a day (lunch and dinner), utilities, scheduled transportation, 24-hour staffing, weekly housekeeping, social activities, and use of all community areas. Telephone and cable TV are extra. An assisted living wing provides additional personal care services.

AMENITIES

Apartments are attractive, with high ceilings. Each apartment has an emergency call system. The community amenities are appealing and include an outdoor swimming pool, lounges, a billiards room, activities, and a library. The dining room is elegant.

REVIEWER'S NOTES

Campana del Rio is a new development with an elegant, comfortable feeling. It is located in an area of Tucson that we personally like—the north foothills. The facility is pleasing to the eye and the staff were very professional. Residents are between 55 and 85 years of age.

THE CASCADES

Rent

201 North Jessica

Tucson, AZ 85710

(602) 886-3171

Karla Finch, Marketing

INDEPENDENT LIVING FACILITY

A rental community for adults who desire assisted living amenities. Established in 1978; owned and managed since 1982 by James Mayhen Investments, Inc.

HOUSING TYPES AVAILABLE

Studio and one-bedroom apartments available in a five-story, high-rise elevator building organized in four wings with a central main entrance. All apartments are one level. The one bedrooms are 500 sq ft; studios are 288 sq ft. The building has a bright attractive lobby, and wide corridors lead to the apartments. The apartments have balconies and are well laid out with wide doorways and walk-in showers with built-in seats and safety bars.

NUMBER OF SITES/UNITS

240 apartments.

LOCATION

The Cascades is located in southeast Tucson in a well-developed area convenient to shopping, churches, and hospitals. Park Mall Shopping Center and St. Joseph's Hospital are a few blocks away. This area is a solid section of Tucson which continues to have new development.

REQUIREMENTS/RESTRICTIONS

Usually 65 or older; small pets are allowed.

FEES

Studio apartments rent for $545 per month; one bedroom from $725 to $750 per month depending on location. Most amenities are included in the monthly rent except for meals, which are offered either a la carte or under several meal plans, the most common of which is three meals per day for $170 a month.

AMENITIES

The Cascades offers a variety of assisted living and catered services including shared dining, housekeeping, 24-hour emergency call service in rooms, transportation, and an extensive program of activities and personal services. Amenities provided are a swimming pool, billiards and game room, arts and crafts room, reading area, beauty salon, and a branch of a local bank that is open two days a week.

REVIEWER'S NOTES

The Cascades is older and on first appearance less elegant than some of the other communities reviewed. However, we were favorably impressed with the feeling of the place, the activities offered, and with Karla Finch, who has worked there since 1981. The average age of residents is just over 80 years. On the day of our visit, the community seemed very busy.

FAIRFIELD'S LA CHOLLA HILLS

8700 North La Cholla Boulevard

Tucson, AZ 85741

(602) 742-6291; (800) 223-9621

Buy

INDEPENDENT LIVING FACILITY

A planned retirement community established in 1985. Developed by Fairfield.

HOUSING TYPES AVAILABLE

Single-family homes and duplexes (townhomes) with 15 different types ranging from one bedroom to three bedrooms. The community is 90 percent sold out, however, and only four types are available as new construction. Resales are available. Square footage ranges from 740 to 2050 depending on the model. The homes are all single level with a southwestern territorial design. The homes have a distinctive red brick (block) look to them, with a flat-roof type design (they are not totally flat but appear to be).

NUMBER OF SITES/UNITS

389 single family homes and duplexes. Currently only 16 new units are unsold; resales are available.

LOCATION

La Cholla is located on the northwest side of Tucson overlooking the Tucson National Golf Club. Although the area is well developed, it still has a rural and less congested feel to it than other parts of Tucson. All types of services and amenities are within close proximity. However, a car is needed.

REQUIREMENTS/RESTRICTIONS

One resident in a household must be at least 55.

FEES

Available new single-family homes and duplexes start at $54,900 and climb to $109,900. Certain lots have added premiums. Residents pay homeowner association fees of $36 per month for the use of all recreational facilities, common landscaping (which is extensive), street maintenance, and security.

AMENITIES

La Cholla Hills has two recreational areas located on opposite ends of the development. Both have pools and clubhouse activities. The recreational areas provide a pleasant atmosphere, but are not overwhelming as they are in some other communities we have seen. There is no golf in the community. However, several championship golf courses are within a few miles. Area amenities include nearby hospitals and doctors' offices, local supermarkets, a mall, churches, and local entertainment.

REVIEWER'S NOTES

La Cholla Hills is a beautifully landscaped and maintained community. It is hilly, which adds interest but may be a disadvantage if a person is handicapped. It is a small, self-contained community that provides a sense of privacy.

THE FOUNTAINS AT LA CHOLLA

Rent

2001 West Rudasill Road

Tucson, AZ 85704

(602) 797-2001

INDEPENDENT LIVING FACILITY

A rental community for adults desiring a full-service catered lifestyle. Established in December 1987 and developed, owned and managed by The Elan Group, a local Tucson development company.

HOUSING TYPES AVAILABLE

One- and two-bedroom apartments in a three-story complex divided into three wings with four courtyards. Apartments range from 416 to over 865 sq ft. There are four models to choose from. The main entrance and clubhouse are unusually elegant. The corridors are wide and wheelchairs and carts are acceptable as long as a resident can live independently. The apartments are pleasant, with wide halls and excellent bathrooms with wide doors, walk-in showers, and guardrails.

NUMBER OF SITES/UNITS

260 apartments.

LOCATION

The Fountains is located on the northern edge of Tucson. This is a less congested part of the city but still very convenient to area amenities and services. Directly across from The Fountains is HCA Senora Desert Hospital. Northwest Hospital and two nursing facilities are one block away. Recreation, shopping, churches, and other amenities are close by.

REQUIREMENTS/RESTRICTIONS

Minimum age 62 (spouse can be younger); pets under 20 pounds allowed.

FEES

One-bedroom apartments from $820 to $975 per month; two bedrooms from $1230 to $1390. The charge for an additional person is $300 per month. Services included in the monthly fee are one meal per day (lunch or dinner), housekeeping every other week, scheduled transportation, utilities, continental breakfast, 24-hour staffing, wellness program, and the use of all community areas. Telephone and cable TV are extra.

AMENITIES

Apartments have emergency call systems. Community amenities include an expansive, elegant clubhouse with a convenience store and beauty shop, branch bank, scheduled transportation, elegant dining, a swimming pool, horseshoes, shuffleboard, billiards, and rooms for activities and arts and handicrafts.

REVIEWER'S NOTES

This is an impressive retirement community where the developers seem to have paid careful attention to small but important details affecting their residents. The atmosphere is elegant and not overpowering. The location is in the northern, less congested part of Tucson but still close to needed services and amenities. The average age of residents is 70 to 80.

RINCON COUNTRY RV RESORT

RINCON COUNTRY EAST RV RESORT

8989 East Escalante

Tucson, AZ 85730

(602) 886-8431

RINCON COUNTRY WEST RV RESORT

4555 South Mission Road

Tucson, AZ 85714

(602) 294-5608; (800) RV2-PARK

INDEPENDENT LIVING FACILITY

Rincon Country East and West are two RV parks for short-term visitors and year-round residents. Family owned and operated by the O'Leary family since 1971.

HOUSING TYPES AVAILABLE

RV and park model trailers are permitted. Standard lots are 31 feet wide and 45 feet deep; value-plus lots are 33 feet wide and 45 or 50 feet deep. Premium lots are 35 feet wide and 50 feet deep. Residents add patios.

NUMBER OF SITES/UNITS

2 sites; East, 460 lots; West, 1100 lots.

LOCATION

Rincon Country West is located on the south side of Tucson near the intersection of Ajo Road and I-19 on Mission Road near the famous San Xavier Del Bac Spanish Mission. Rincon Country East is located in southeast Tucson, just east of Davis Monthan Air Force Base, in a mixed residential area. Both locations are within five miles of Tucson services such as hospitals, doctors' offices, shopping, churches, and recreation.

REQUIREMENTS/RESTRICTIONS

Adults only. Pets allowed in pet section of parks.

FEES

Daily space rates are $15 to $18; weekly, $89 to $104; monthly, $200 to $295; and annual, $1200 to $1575 depending on the site and lot selected. Rates are for two people and are subject to a rental tax. There is an additional charge of $1 per day, $25 per month, or $150 per year per additional person. Electricity and cable TV are included in daily and weekly rates. Phone hookup is additional.

AMENITIES

Rincon Country offers every type of club and social group you can imagine—from golf groups, to hiking, to arts and crafts. If you have an interest, it is very likely that there is a group activity in that area at Rincon Country. Other amenities include swimming pools, a Jacuzzi, laundry facilities, tennis, shuffleboard, a library, card rooms, crafts, lapidary, an amateur radio room, sewing, and 24-hour security.

REVIEWER'S NOTES

We were especially impressed with Marilyn Thompson, the manager of Rincon Country East, and all the on-going clubs and activities. At the East location, over 90 percent of the lots are rented on an annual basis and there is a definite community spirit. The area surrounding Rincon East is mixed, but the park is an oasis worth considering. Rincon West is more modern and still under construction.

SADDLEBROOKE

64518 East SaddleBrooke Boulevard

Tucson, AZ 85737

(602) 791-7464

Buy

INDEPENDENT LIVING FACILITY

A planned retirement community established in 1986. Developed by Edward Robson-Sun Lakes Co., Sun Lakes, Arizona.

HOUSING TYPES AVAILABLE

There are single-family homes with two or three bedrooms in 14 models and several different room elevations to choose from. Square footage ranges from 1361 sq ft to 2495 depending on the model. The homes are all single level with mission tile roofs, many with cathedral ceilings and open kitchens and dining rooms. The homes have an attractive feeling to them.

NUMBER OF SITES/UNITS

Currently 400 lots sold, with about 200 residents. This is a new community with plans to grow to 2000 homes.

LOCATION

The location is spectacular, rural, and somewhat remote. To reach SaddleBrooke, drive up Rt. 89 into Oro Valley. You enter a very rural, sparsely populated area that continues for 10 to 15 miles until you pass through the small town of Catalina. You will drive about two miles farther, going through part of Eagle Crest Ranch (a working cattle ranch), and up over a small hill. There you have your first view of SaddleBrooke, which is located in a valley below the Catalina mountains. The nearest hospital is about 16 miles away, and many other services are equally distant.

REQUIREMENTS/RESTRICTIONS

Residents must be 40 and over.

FEES

New single-family homes start at $91,850 for a two bedroom, two bath and climb to $206,895, depending on the model and lot chosen. Homeowners' fees are $300 per year per household for all recreational facilities (except golf), maintenance of common areas, and a security patrol. SaddleBrooke has a lot-purchase plan that people interested in preretirement advance purchase should look into. This plan allows you to purchase your lot and take up to two years to begin construction of your home.

AMENITIES

Community amenities include a new $5 million recreation center with swimming, tennis, a very elegant dining room and other amenities that contribute to a country-club atmosphere. There is also a private 18-hole championship golf course only for residents; fees are $300 per year or $12 daily. Because of SaddleBrooke's rural location, other services such as supermarkets, malls, churches, and entertainment are at least 8 to 10 miles away. The fire department is four miles away but a substation is scheduled to be completed by the end of 1989.

REVIEWER'S NOTES

The scenery and setting of SaddleBrooke are spectacular and definitely should be seen by anyone looking for a small, rural community in an elegant setting. SaddleBrooke is owned and was developed by Edward Robson, the very successful developer of Sun Lakes near Phoenix. The climate is somewhat cooler than Tucson because of the altitude (3300 ft). The homes themselves are attractive with a very open feeling.

SANTA CATALINA VILLAS

Rent

7500 North Calle Sin Envidia

Tucson, AZ 85718

(602) 742-6242

INDEPENDENT LIVING FACILITY

A rental community for adults in a resort-style setting. Established in 1988 and owned and operated by Caring Communities, San Francisco, California.

HOUSING TYPES AVAILABLE

Studio and one- and two-bedroom apartments available in 15 two-story elevator buildings that open to the outside to covered walkways. Because each building has only four to 10 apartments, the units are like villas. Studio apartments have 492 sq ft; one bedroom, one bath, 602 to 726 sq ft; one bedroom, two bath, 727 sq ft; and two bedroom, two bath, 905 to 1455 sq ft. All apartments have patios or balconies. We were not able to see an apartment during our visit so we cannot comment on the interiors. However, all have 24-hour emergency call systems, full kitchens, and oversized bathrooms.

NUMBER OF SITES/UNITS

164 apartments; 15 provide more comprehensive assisted living services.

LOCATION

Santa Catalina Villas is located in the foothills of Santa Catalina Mountains north of Tucson in the very exclusive Rancho Sin Vacas housing community. The location is absolutely spectacular. The hilly area may be a drawback to some with walking disabilities; however, the developer has worked carefully to make the community very accessible. The location is somewhat removed from major shopping and medical services, which are approximately 10 to 15 minutes away.

REQUIREMENTS/RESTRICTIONS

Mature adults, no minimum age. Pets allowed.

FEES

Studio apartments rent for $700 to $900 per month; one bedroom, one bath, $800 to $1500; one bedroom, two bath, $1200 to $1400; and two bedroom, two bath, $1500 to $2900. There is an additional person charge of $295 per month. These fees include utilities, except telephone and electricity, 24-hour security, 20 meals per month, housekeeping, weekly flat linen service, cable TV hookup and basic service, transportation, fitness/wellness center membership, health checkups, social activities, and the use of all community facilities. Santa Catalina Villas also provides apartments for winter visitors. One-bedroom furnished apartments start at $1445 per month, including electricity and the use of community services. Meals and housekeeping are on an a la carte basis. There is a two-month minimum.

AMENITIES

The community itself is strikingly beautiful in terms of both the construction and the setting. Amenities include an elegant clubhouse, dining, a swimming pool and Jacuzzi, a billiard room, convenience shop, crafts and hobbies, a health club, a health/wellness program, a photographic darkroom, 24-hour security, banking, a beauty/barber salon, and extensive social activities. Santa Catalina also stresses its Wellness Center (operated in conjunction with the University of Arizona) with an RN on duty as well as La Rosa Assisted Living Center for people needing more assisted living services.

REVIEWER'S NOTES

Santa Catalina Villas without a doubt is located in one of the most beautiful settings in the Southwest. If you are looking for a spectacular Southwest setting in a resort-style community with extensive amenities and services, Santa Catalina is a must visit. The average age of residents is currently in the late 70s but we believe this community could appeal to younger mature adults as well.

SUN CITY TUCSON

Buy

13990 North Desert Butte Drive

Tucson, AZ 85737

(602) 620-6800; (800) 422-8483

INDEPENDENT LIVING FACILITY

A planned retirement community established in 1986. Developed and owned by Del Webb Corporation, Inc.

HOUSING TYPES AVAILABLE

Single-family homes, all single story with mission tile roofing. Most homes have two bedrooms although there are a few with three (or a den/family room). Square footage for the single family homes ranges from 1035 to 2328 depending on the model. Sun City Tucson has 10 models to choose from and there is a semicustom program that, for additional cost, allows the buyer to make changes in the model selected.

NUMBER OF SITES/UNITS

Currently 1000 residents with 650 houses sold. This is a new community with plans to grow to 2500 houses.

LOCATION

The location can best be described as beautiful and rural; some would say remote. Sun City Tucson is located in Oro Valley to the northwest of Tucson at a slightly higher altitude and overlooking the Catalina Mountains. It is adjacent to Rancho Vistoso, a new master-planned community for families. It is rural in that the nearest hospital is 12 miles away and many services are equally distant, although a convenience market is on site. You are approximately 45 minutes from the Tucson airport and 30 minutes from downtown Tucson.

REQUIREMENTS/RESTRICTIONS

One resident in household must be at least 55 years of age.

FEES

New single-family homes (including lot) with two bedrooms and two baths begin at $96,300 and climb to $183,800 for the largest model (2328 sq ft), which has a den or optional third bedroom and an Arizona room. Homeowners' fees covering service for common area landscaping and recreation facilities (except golf) are $270 per year for household of two. Del Webb offers a deferred purchase plan for buyers who want to lock in a price and move in later (subject to restrictions/conditions). The management also offers vacation specials that allow you to stay at a garden villa home and experience living in the community. Rates vary with the season. For more information call (800) 433-9611.

AMENITIES

Del Webb communities are world-renowned for their amenities, and this is no exception. A major recreation center built for $5 million offers every conceivable activity from swimming to boccie ball to miniature golf to arts and crafts. One 18-hole championship golf course is located in the community. Daily fees are about $15 per day. Because of Sun City Tucson's rural location amenities such as supermarkets, malls, churches, and other entertainment are at least five to seven miles away, except for an on-site convenience store.

REVIEWER'S NOTES

This is a beautiful area of Arizona. If you are looking for scenery, fewer crowds, and a more rural setting, this could be for you. The developers expect this area to grow significantly, but that is anyone's guess. Now it is beautiful and uncrowded, but it seems somewhat remote. If you are not bothered by the seclusion, the other attractions will certainly excite you. The scenery is truly beautiful, temperatures are somewhat cooler, and the unique Del Webb approach makes their communities very appealing. The houses themselves are open and light but with fairly low ceilings, which give some a more cozy feeling.

SWAN LAKE ESTATES

4550 North Flowing Wells Road

Tucson, AZ

(602) 887-9292

INDEPENDENT LIVING FACILITY

Adult mobile (manufactured) home community established in 1971. Managed by Jim and Josephine Walsh since 1973.

HOUSING TYPES AVAILABLE

Mobile/manufactured preowned (resale) homes (single- and double-wide) with lots available. Prices range from $10,000 to $40,000, depending on the model and lot selected. No new lots/sales available (only resales).

NUMBER OF SITES/UNITS

278

LOCATION

Swan Lake Estates is located in northwest Tucson in one of the older and less congested parts of the city. The location is very convenient to hospitals, doctors, churches, shopping, and all Tucson has to offer. You are also not far from Interstate 10—a plus because Tucson can become quite congested.

REQUIREMENTS/RESTRICTIONS

55 or older. Pets in certain areas.

FEES

Monthly rental for homesites ranges from $220 to $270 per month depending on the size and location. Rent includes water, sewer, garbage pickup, and the use of recreational facilities.

AMENITIES

Community amenities include a very nice clubhouse for social activities, a swimming pool, shuffleboard courts, and arts and crafts. There is an extensive monthly social calendar.

REVIEWER'S NOTES

Swan Lakes Estates is one of the most attractive and more established manufactured home communities we have visited. In the center of the community is a beautiful lake where you can go fishing. The management is very stable and the community itself is beautifully maintained and landscaped.

TRAILS WEST

8401 South Kolb Road

Tucson, AZ 85706

(602) 574-0298

INDEPENDENT LIVING FACILITY

A planned manufactured (mobile) home community for mature adults. Established in 1985 and owned and operated by a private investor group from Michigan.

HOUSING TYPES AVAILABLE

New manufactured home models offered for sale by dealers and resale homes are available. Both single- and double-wide homes are available.

NUMBER OF SITES/UNITS

442 sites (spaces).

LOCATION

Trails West is located on the southeast edge of Tucson just off I-10 and directly adjacent to Voyager RV Resort. The area is rural and most of the land near the community (except Voyager) is undeveloped. Since this is not part of the city of Tucson, services such as fire and police are provided by the county. Other services, including hospitals, shopping, and churches, are about 10 minutes away, primarily to the north and northeast. The Tucson airport is about 10 minutes away.

REQUIREMENTS/RESTRICTIONS

55 and older. One pet allowed up to 30 pounds.

FEES

Manufactured homes available new or for resale ranging from $20,000 to $60,000 depending on the model and installation fees. New homes are sold by individual dealers; resales are by owners or their agents. Monthly lease rates for two persons are $204 for single-wide spaces and $214 for double wide. The lease includes water, sewer, cable TV wiring, garbage pickup, 24-hour security, and use of all community facilities. Electric, gas, telephone, and cable fees are additional.

AMENITIES

Community amenities include 24-hour security, a clubhouse with a swimming pool, billiard room, card room, library, shuffleboard court, laundry facilities, and planned social and recreational activities.

REVIEWER'S NOTES

Trails West is a pleasant, well-maintained manufactured home community in a rural setting. If you visit, try to talk to Ed, a resident who works in security and is very knowledgeable about the community, or to Richard Vaughn, Property Manager.

VOYAGER RV RESORT

8701 South Kolb Road

Tucson, AZ 85706

(602) 746-2000; (800) 424-9191

INDEPENDENT LIVING FACILITY

Voyager RV Resort is an adult RV park for both short-term and year-round residents. The park is owned and operated by local private owners and was established in 1984.

HOUSING TYPES AVAILABLE

RV and park model trailers are permitted; lots rent on a daily, weekly, monthly, and annual basis.

NUMBER OF SITES/UNITS

1100 sites/lots.

LOCATION

Voyager RV Resort is located on the southeast edge of Tucson just off I-10. The area is rural and most of the land near the resort is undeveloped. Since the resort is not in incorporated Tucson, fire and police are provided by the county. Services such as hospitals, major shopping, and churches are about 10 minutes away, as is the Tucson airport.

REQUIREMENTS/RESTRICTIONS

Adult RV park. Pets allowed.

FEES

Daily space fees are $18 plus tax and include electric; weekly fees are $110 plus tax and include electric; monthly fees are $350; and annual fees are $1645 to $1695. Monthly and annual fees do not include electricity. All rates include water, sewer, garbage collection, free basic cable TV, 24-hour security, social activities, and the use of all amenities. Rates are based on two persons.

AMENITIES

The Voyager RV Resort is one of the largest and most comprehensive of the RV resorts in Arizona. Community amenities include two heated swimming pools, laundry, two therapy pools, saunas, tennis, miniature golf, shuffleboard, and horseshoes. There are very extensive planned social activities, arts and crafts facilities, educational classes, exercise programs, dancing, and church services. There is also a restaurant and a convenience/general store on site.

REVIEWER'S NOTES

Voyager is best described as truly a community unto itself. Everything a community could possibly offer is here in this lovely RV resort; described by some as the "Sun City" of RV resorts. In addition, many local Tucson attractions are only a short drive away.

NEVADA

LAS VEGAS AND HENDERSON, NV

Las Vegas and Henderson are located at the southern edge of Nevada, which borders Arizona, Utah, and California. The cities are located in a large valley surrounded by mountains.

The first settlers arrived in 1855, but this century has seen the major development of this area. In the 1930s the federal government decided to build Hoover Dam just 30 miles from Las Vegas. Later, legal gambling transformed this small community into a world famous resort area.

The gambling casinos and resorts are truly spectacular, and for anyone who enjoys gambling this area is a must. The casinos, nightlife, restaurants, and recreational amenities are extensive and cater to people of all ages. The casinos are known to allow RVers to park overnight in their parking lots.

Outside the casino areas, the cities have a southwestern feeling to them. The population is growing rapidly. The area now has over 700,000 residents, with of course thousands of visitors each week. Although there are excellent health services, retirement options and services are somewhat limited.

Residents of Nevada neither pay state income nor inheritance tax, and the state subsidizes real property taxes and rents of people 62 and older who meet certain income criteria.

Average temperatures for January range from 55 to 32 degrees, and for July 105 to 76 degrees. Average annual precipitation is nine inches.

For more information on the Las Vegas-Henderson area, contact the Las Vegas Chamber of Commerce, 2301 East Sahara Avenue, Las Vegas, NV 89104, or call (702) 457-4664.

LAUGHLIN, NV/BULLHEAD CITY, AZ

Laughlin and Bullhead City lie on either side of the Colorado River at the southernmost tip of Nevada bordering Arizona. There is a bridge linking the two cities, as well as ferry service provided by Laughlin's casinos. While Laughlin provides 24-hour-a-day action at the casinos, Bullhead City in Arizona supplies most of the residential housing. This is said to be the fastest growing area in Arizona.

The warm, dry climate in addition to the water sports and gambling casinos attract many visitors, especially in the winter. Average temperatures in July range from 108.2 to 79.1 degrees; in January from 62.2 to 44.8 degrees. Average yearly rainfall is 4.19 inches. The population is approximately 25,000, up from 10,363 in 1980. The main economic activities in the area are tourism, hydroelectric generators, and the eight casinos on the Nevada side.

Laughlin's casinos provide retirees with free or low-cost RV parking; some have full hook-ups available. During winter months one sees as many RVs in the parking lots as cars! For those looking at this area as a more long-term or permanent residence the casinos appear to hire many retirees for part-time positions.

Recreational facilities include fishing and water sports on the Colorado River and nearby Mohave and Mead lakes, casino gambling and shows, and golf at Chaparral Country Club. The Black Mountain Range to the east is interesting for hiking, taking photographs, exploring old ghost towns, and hunting.

This area is located about 230 miles from Phoenix and 90 miles from Las Vegas. As with most towns on the Colorado River, there are numerous RV parks for winter visitors (21 parks with a total of 2463 sites). Property owners in Bullhead City pay $10.62 per $100 assessed valuation. Nevada residents pay no state income tax, which is a plus to many retirees.

Bullhead City is currently experiencing a building boom and there is quite a bit of speculation by developers on available land. Many expect this area to continue to be one of the fastest growing in Arizona through the 1990's.

Services in the area include one hospital, one extended care facility, over 35 physicians and dentists, several banks and savings and loans, and shopping. There is also a small airport that handles regional direct carriers as well as private planes. For further information contact: Bullhead Area Chamber of Commerce, PO Box 66, Bullhead City, AZ 86430, or call (602) 754-4121.

CAMLU RETIREMENT APARTMENTS

Rent

4255 Spencer Street

Las Vegas, NV 89119

(702) 732-0652

Shirley Wilson, Manager

INDEPENDENT LIVING FACILITY

A rental community with assisted living amenities. Established in 1953 and owned and operated by Camlu Corporation, San Diego, which operates eleven other similar facilities throughout the Southwest.

HOUSING TYPES AVAILABLE

Studio, one-bedroom, and a few two-bedroom apartments in a two-story complex. Studio apartments are approximately 325 sq ft; one bedrooms, 435 sq ft. Apartments are all one level and comfortable, with good windows for outside light. All apartments open to the inside, so that you do not have to go outside to reach the dining room or other areas. The apartments have good accessibility for the disabled and 24-hour emergency call systems. They do not have full kitchens (no stoves); however, with the meal plans this may not be necessary. You can have a microwave.

NUMBER OF SITES/UNITS

74 apartments.

LOCATION

Camlu is located on the eastern side of Las Vegas in an older residential community. The location is a major selling point; it is close to all types of amenities and services but still residential. Hospitals, doctors, supermarkets, shopping, churches, and entertainment are all within a few miles. The airport is approximately 15-20 minutes away.

REQUIREMENTS/RESTRICTIONS

Minimum age 55; no pets allowed.

FEES

One-bedroom unfurnished apartments rent for $840 per month; studio apartments for $705 per month. There is a second person charge of $200 per month. Services included in the monthly rent are three meals a day, all utilities, weekly housekeeping, scheduled transportation, 24-hour staffing, and social activities. Telephone and cable TV are extra.

AMENITIES

The community itself offers pleasant surroundings with garden areas and an attractive TV lounge, library, and arts and crafts rooms. There is a beauty salon on-site. There is no swimming pool.

REVIEWER'S NOTES

From the moment I arrived the receptionist (who is also a resident) and the manager, Shirley Wilson, made me feel very welcome. The community is comfortable but unpretentious. The surroundings and garden areas, which are pleasant and well maintained, add much to the overall feeling. The average age of residents is 75 to 85.

DEL WEBB'S SUN CITY LAS VEGAS

Buy

PO Box 82040, 9119 Garden View Drive

Las Vegas, NV 89180-2024

(702) 363-5454; (800) 843-4848

INDEPENDENT LIVING FACILITY

A master-planned active adult community established in 1988 by Del Webb Corporation, owner/developer of Sun City, Sun City West, and Sun City Vistoso in Arizona.

HOUSING TYPES AVAILABLE

Single-family homes in seven different floor plans ranging in size from 1086 to 2491 sq ft. All but the largest two models have two bedrooms and two baths. The largest two models have three bedrooms and two baths. All have two-car garages. Duplex models are 1143, 1327, and 1731 sq ft in size, with two bedrooms and two baths. Garden villas (townhouses) consist of four connecting units with three different floor plans available. Their square footage ranges from 1062 to 1316 including one-and-a-half car garages. All models are single level with covered patios. Architecturally all models share the light and open Southwest style. Even the smaller models feel spacious and are well-designed for comfortable living.

NUMBER OF SITES/UNITS

3100 homes on 1050 acres in Phase I. Currently about half the sites have been sold. Phase II, which is in the planning stage, will provide an additional 2800 homes.

LOCATION

Sun City is eight miles northwest of downtown Las Vegas. At present the community is somewhat isolated from other housing and services. It is part of Howard Hughes Properties, a 25,000-acre site; plans are to develop this area with all necessary services and conveniences. Del Webb's parcel will be master-plan developed. Shopping is available within a five-mile radius, and a major hospital is within a 15-minute drive.

REQUIREMENTS/RESTRICTIONS

Minimum age, 55 for one household resident. No children under 19 to be permanent residents. Pets allowed.

FEES

All home prices include the lot. Single-family homes range from $87,400 to $196,000 with prices in between ranging from $96,100 to $171,600. There are a wide variety of upgrades and optional features available to customize each home. Duplexes, priced at $93,200 and $114,700, can also be customized at additional cost. Garden villas are $81,700, $103,900, and $111,200, with customizing features available. All homeowners pay an annual $250 recreation fee per home. Duplex owners pay an additional $97 monthly that covers water, building insurance, exterior maintenance, landscaping maintenance, and capital improvements. Garden villa owners' monthly fee is $85 and covers the same items as the duplex owners' fee. Golf course users have two options: Pay as you play or pay $500 annually plus $1 for every nine holes played.

AMENITIES

There is an 18-hole professional golf course on the grounds. Three recreation buildings house extensive recreational and social rooms, eating establishments, crafts rooms, and a sports center. There is a swimming pool and a spa. This recreation complex is at the center of the community.

REVIEWER'S NOTES

Del Webb has again put their years of expertise into a new community. This location already promises to be as popular as the three Sun City communities. This facility is unique in Las Vegas and should be visited if you are at all interested in the area. Building in the surrounding area is on the rise and this should soon lessen the feeling of isolation. Tax advantages in Nevada can be especially attractive to seniors. If you are in the vicinity, it is well worth a visit.

THE MEADOWS

2900 Valley View

Las Vegas, NV 89102

(702) 876-3660

INDEPENDENT LIVING FACILITY

A community of mobile/manufactured homes for active adults, established in 1974. The current owner is Las Vegas Meadows, Ltd.

HOUSING TYPES AVAILABLE

Mobile homes available for resale are offered periodically either through the individual owners or local real estate agencies. There are no new lots available. The facility management does not handle sales but may be able to direct interested parties to local realtors. All homes in this park meet high standards for upkeep and improvements. These standards are enforced and provide for a uniform appearance that indicates permanence. There is no feeling of "trailer-park" transience. Since homes vary in size, there is a choice for potential buyers depending on availability.

NUMBER OF SITES/UNITS

332 lots with homes.

LOCATION

The Meadows is located on the west side of Las Vegas near medical facilities, all types of shopping, and the Las Vegas "strip."

REQUIREMENTS/RESTRICTIONS

Minimum age 55. Children under 18 may visit with resident supervision. Pets permitted with leash laws enforced.

FEES

All homes are on rental lots. Lot rental ranges from $200 to $300 monthly. Home prices range from $25,000 to over $55,000, depending on the model and real estate market at the time of purchase. The Meadows has a consistently small number of homes listed with realtors at any given time, but there were several homes for sale "by owner" with signs in the window. A drive through the facility should provide a few more options to supplement realtor listings.

AMENITIES

The Meadows offers an excellent location convenient to all Las Vegas services and activities. The recreation center is large and well maintained in a parklike setting. Security begins at the gate with a guard who checks visitors. Facilities include two heated pools with a spa, tennis courts, a sauna, an exercise room, game rooms, a billiard room, a ballroom, a library, and picnic areas. There is also a full activities calendar offering something for everyone.

REVIEWER'S NOTES

The Meadows is well maintained and has a very stable feeling. All homes are well cared for on the outside and there is a sense of community pride about the facility. Even though there are several other facilities of this type in the area, only a few homes were for sale. Residents must like living here. We recommend contacting the management for more detailed information and names of local realtors.

MONTARA MEADOWS

Rent

3150 East Tropicana Avenue

Las Vegas, NV 89121

(702) 435-3150

Murray Rosenblum

INDEPENDENT LIVING FACILITY

An active adult community with many amenities for a "catered" lifestyle, established in 1987 by Murray Rosenblum, the current owner and manager.

HOUSING TYPES AVAILABLE

Studio, one-bedroom, and two-bedroom apartments are available. Approximate square footage ranges from 450 to 740. All units have one bath. The apartments are of sufficient size to be comfortable and offer modern upgraded features. As three meals a day are provided, units have only kitchenettes.

NUMBER OF SITES/UNITS

174 apartments.

LOCATION

Located in east central Las Vegas the community is convenient to all services. The immediate area is a mixture of residential and small businesses.

REQUIREMENTS/RESTRICTIONS

No specific requirement. The average age is over 65.

FEES

Montara Meadows includes virtually everything in the monthly fee. A studio apartment (single occupancy) is $1025; one bedroom, $1225 to $1325 (single); and two bedroom, $1675 to $1775 (double). Add $335 per month for a second person in one-bedroom units. Fees include three meals daily, served restaurant style, scheduled transportation, many scheduled activities, exercise classes, 24-hour emergency call service, and the use of all recreational facilities. Utilities and housekeeping are also included.

AMENITIES

Meals, activities, and services are included in the monthly fee. Other amenities include a swimming pool and putting green. The common areas and grounds are well maintained and elegantly furnished.

REVIEWER'S NOTES

Montara Meadows provides many desirable amenities and presents them in an elegant manner. The services are well thought out and appealing to those who desire freedom from day-to-day chores. To us it exemplified the best of full service. Some people may find this to be more service than they need, while others may well appreciate the "pampered" lifestyle this community offers.

PARADISE COVE

Rent

4330 Eastern Avenue

Las Vegas, NV 89119

(702) 369-1552

Nan Thomas, Marketing Director

INDEPENDENT LIVING FACILITY

A rental community for independent adults desiring a range of services and amenities. Established in 1984, owned and managed by Heritage Management Corporation of America.

HOUSING TYPES AVAILABLE

Apartments are single level, whether ground floor or second story. All units have a patio or balcony, and there are conveniently located elevators for second-floor residents. Walkways are open but covered. Studio apartments offer 520 sq ft of space; one bedroom, 624 sq ft; two bedroom, one bath, 884 sq ft; and two bedroom, two bath, 1050 sq ft. All apartments have kitchens and walk-in closets. The studio apartment is larger than average.

NUMBER OF SITES/UNITS

108 apartments.

LOCATION

The community is centrally located in Las Vegas and convenient to hospital, shopping, churches, the airport, and casinos.

REQUIREMENTS/RESTRICTIONS

Adults, no specific age minimum. No pets.

FEES

Monthly rates for single occupancy are as follows: studio, $710; one-bedroom apartment, $850; two bedroom, $975; and deluxe two bedroom, $1090, with an additional $200 monthly for a second person. Rent includes the noon meal, local scheduled transportation, weekly maid service, recreation and activities, security guard, security call systems in apartments, water, sewer, and trash pickup.

AMENITIES

Amenities include a tastefully decorated dining room, common areas, and lounges. There is a pool with a spa in the center courtyard. Transportation is provided to shopping and banking. Casinos send scheduled buses on a regular basis to shuttle residents to and from their facilities. Scheduled activities vary daily.

REVIEWER'S NOTES

Paradise Cove provides moderately priced accommodations and services to those desiring a central Las Vegas location. The apartments are spacious and have good storage. It is one of only a few exclusively retiree apartment complexes in the area. We found it more than acceptable.

THREE CROWNS MOBILE MANOR

867 North Lamb Boulevard

Las Vegas, NV 89110

(702) 452-5720

INDEPENDENT LIVING FACILITY

A community of mobile (manufactured) homes for active adults. Established in 1972 by Boston Group, Salt Lake City, Utah. They are the current owners.

HOUSING TYPES AVAILABLE

Mobile homes for resale only. Models vary in size and availability is limited. Sales are by owner or listed with local realtors. Most of the homes are over five years old, but the general condition appears to be very good. Facility managers do not handle sales.

NUMBER OF SITES/UNITS

265 lots.

LOCATION

Located on the north side of Las Vegas, the community is convenient to shopping, the city bus, and casinos. Medical facilities are three blocks away.

REQUIREMENTS/RESTRICTIONS

Minimum age 55. Small pets are permitted.

FEES

Monthly rent charged for spaces is $282. It includes water, sewer, garbage, and use of the recreational facilities. Home prices vary with the home and real estate market in general. The typical range is from $28,000 to $55,000.

AMENITIES

Facilities include a heated pool, Jacuzzi, laundry, saunas, an exercise room, card and game rooms, a ballroom, a library, and a billiard room. There is RV parking and guest parking available. The planned social calendar is very full, with various activities. Casinos run shuttle buses to and from Three Crowns.

REVIEWER'S NOTES

Three Crowns is obviously very stable and the residents seem reluctant to leave. The residents appear to enjoy the sense of community. Sign-up sheets for activities were full. The look of the community is pleasant and streets are quiet and well lit. If you are interested in a mobile home community in this area, be prepared to wait for vacancies.

VILLA BOREGA

1111 North Lamb Boulevard

Las Vegas, NV 89110

(702) 452-3758

Bill Iverson; Marge Iverson, co-owner/managers

INDEPENDENT LIVING FACILITY

An adult mobile (manufactured) home community built in 1980 by the current co-owners and Mobile Park West.

HOUSING TYPES AVAILABLE

Mobile/manufactured homes with lots still available for new homes, with some resales on the market as well. All homes must be set up so that no signs of "mobility" appear. Only double- and triple-wide homes are permitted. New homes available from local dealers/manufacturers can cost from $25,000 to $65,000, depending on the model selected. (Remember to ask about delivery and setup charges, which may or may not be included). Resale home cost will be in the same range.

NUMBER OF SITES/UNITS

293 lots.

LOCATION

The community is located in the northern part of Las Vegas, which is convenient to all medical facilities, shopping, services, churches, and casinos. Villa Borega is near a city bus line but your own car is usually necessary.

REQUIREMENTS/RESTRICTIONS

Minimum age 55 for one household member. Pets are permitted but must be contained on your own property.

FEES

Monthly rental for home sites from $289 to $343, depending on size and location. Rent includes water, sewer, garbage, and use of recreational facilities.

AMENITIES

The recreation center is large, consisting of three buildings and provides a pool, tennis courts, crafts room, a library, and social rooms. It is clean and well furnished for various activities. The co-owner/managers have an office there.

REVIEWER'S NOTES

Villa Borega is in a good location and is not in an overdeveloped area. There are still lots available for those wishing to select their own new homes and there is a wide variety of features to choose from. All the existing homes are well kept and the community is attractive.

CHEYENNE RETIREMENT CAMPUS

Rent

2860 East Cheyenne

North Las Vegas, NV 89030

(702) 644-7777

INDEPENDENT LIVING FACILITY

An assisted living facility, with dormitory-style housing for older seniors requiring assistance but not skilled nursing. Established in 1987, it is a licensed residential care facility.

HOUSING TYPES AVAILABLE

Accommodations consist of standard dormitory-size rooms with lavatory, refrigerator, and shared or private bath. Semiprivate and private rooms are available. All rooms are furnished with a bed (or beds) and a dresser. The building is single story with interior hallways.

NUMBER OF SITES/UNITS

125 rooms.

LOCATION

Cheyenne Retirement Campus is in north Las Vegas, approximately 20 minutes from downtown and "The Strip." It is located directly across the street from Clark County Community College. A hospital, doctors' offices, shopping, and gambling establishments are within a five-mile radius.

REQUIREMENTS/RESTRICTIONS

Senior adults. No pets.

FEES

A semiprivate room (for two people) with a shared bath is $685 per month; a private room (single occupancy), $1050 to $1200, depending on the private bath option; and couples (one room), $1200 to $1400. The monthly fee includes three meals daily, housekeeping and linen service, scheduled transportation, recreational activities, and the use of common area lounges. A registered nurse reviews residents' medication on a weekly basis. Every effort is made to assist residents with low incomes to obtain available funds through government-assisted programs (SSI).

AMENITIES

In addition to the amenities included in the monthly fees, personal daily care is available to those desiring additional assistance for $125 monthly. Daily maid service costs an additional $30 per month.

REVIEWER'S NOTES

Cheyenne Retirement Campus seems to cater to individuals in the transition period between active independent living and full nursing care. It provides a homelike environment with security and supervision for those wishing to maintain some level of autonomy. It would not appeal to a healthy, active retiree but perhaps could be considered by an adult child or spouse of someone requiring closer monitoring than can be provided at home. It is included in this book for that reason.

NEW MEXICO

ALBUQUERQUE, NM

Located in north central New Mexico at the base of the Sandia and Manzano Mountains, Albuquerque has a population of 366,750 people (1986). Both ethnically and culturally diverse, the city has taken its flavor from the American Indians, Hispanics, and Anglos that have occupied the area.

Site of the 100-year-old University of New Mexico, the city has a good number of museums, and art galleries and a symphony orchestra. Not far from the university is historic Old Town, the original Spanish settlement of 1706. Today Old Town is famous for its shops, the shady plaza, and the San Felipe Church. Many Santa Fe and Taos artists and craftspersons sell their work in the shops and boutiques of Old Town.

Albuquerque experiences four seasons, but the climate is mild. Snow falls infrequently and does not linger long. Summers are warm and dry with temperatures in the 90s. September and October are ideal months. As with most of the Southwest, lifestyle and dress here are casual. However, there are a number of fine restaurants that are somewhat more formal.

Buildings and homes are built in a distinctive style known as territorial, Santa Fe, or southwestern. Typical of this style is the flat roof, arched entries, exposed beams, and adobe (mud) facades. Unlike most cities in Arizona and Nevada, Albuquerque has a good many mature, tall leafy trees. Housing costs are moderate. Three-bedroom, two-bath homes start at about $55,000; and two-bedroom apartments average about $400 per month. These prices are for general housing.

Retirees do not flock to Albuquerque in the numbers they do to Arizona. This is due in part to the cool winter climate, but the trade-off is the milder summer weather. Winter temperatures in the upper 50s and 60s are not unreasonable, and weighing that against 105 degree plus summers in Phoenix might encourage more retirees to move to New Mexico. For further information, contact the Albuquerque Convention and Visitors Bureau (505) 768-4575.

SANTA FE, NM

Santa Fe is located about 65 miles north of Albuquerque and has a population of approximately 60,000. Founded in 1610 by a Spanish explorer, it became a center for trade and further exploration for the Spanish. Throughout its history it has served as a commercial center, and it is the state's capital. It was the end of the Santa Fe Trail in the 1800s and after that the Santa Fe railroad. Known primarily as the cultural center of the Southwest, it is home to many artisans, artists, and other notable figures in the art world. Each summer thousands flock to hear the Santa Fe Opera and Chamber Music Festival.

Drawing from the ethnic culture of the Indians, Spanish, and Anglos, Santa Fe retains much of its historical flavor. The plaza has been restored to its original state but now houses shops, boutiques, and museums instead of Spanish governors and missionaries. Several churches and chapels dating from the seventeenth century that have been restored are some of the oldest churches in America.

It is said that there are more than 300 days of sunshine each year. At an altitude of 7000 feet, you can expect chilly winters and pleasant summers. The high altitude could pose a health risk to individuals with certain conditions, so it is advisable to consult your physician before deciding on a long stay.

Retirees moving here from outside the area might be categorized as having rather selective tastes. Cultural and intellectual pursuits outnumber all recreational activities here. Retired opera stars, writers, pianists, artists, and philanthropists are numerous in Santa Fe. Home costs almost rival those of New York and choice land can go for as much as $100,000 an acre. The two retirement communities are attractively priced for the area.

While still relaxed, the lifestyle here is somewhat less casual and less "anything goes" than Albuquerque or even Phoenix. Santa Fe has a unique style and spirit that is obvious in its architecture, dress, and cuisine. For further information contact: Santa Fe County, (800) 548-8272. Santa Fe Convention and Visitors Bureau, PO Box 909, Santa Fe, NM 87504-0909, (800) 777-CITY or (505) 984-6760.

CAMLU RETIREMENT APARTMENTS

Rent

12101 Lomas Boulevard, NE

Albuquerque, NM 87112

(505) 298-9976

INDEPENDENT LIVING FACILITY

The staff of this facility would not answer questions or allow us to see anything beyond the reception area. All information was taken from their promotional materials. Camlu Company has been part of the retirement housing business since the early 1950s.

HOUSING TYPES AVAILABLE

Small studio (360 sq ft) and one-bedroom (670 sq ft) apartments without kitchens but with a refrigerator and sink. The building exterior looked to be at least 10 years old and was modest both inside and out. Furnished apartments may be available.

NUMBER OF SITES/UNITS

Information not disclosed; our estimate is 85 to 100 apartments.

LOCATION

Camlu is yet another retirement facility located in northeast Albuquerque. Convenient to hospital, clinics, and other services, these apartments are in a neighborhood containing a mixture of apartment complexes and commercial business. Interstate 40 is very nearby.

REQUIREMENTS/RESTRICTIONS

Information not disclosed.

FEES

Monthly rates for a studio apartment are $678.50 for one person and $882 for two persons. A one bedroom for one person is $918.50; $1122 for two. Fees include three meals daily, utilities, maid services, recreation room use, intercom system to front desk, and social activities.

AMENITIES

From handout information, we gather that the amenities at Camlu are covered under the fee. It would appear from their marketing information that no long-term lease needs to be signed.

REVIEWER'S NOTES

It is difficult to comment on this Camlu facility because of the reception we received. We did discover during visits to other Albuquerque facilities that they do refer people to Camlu if they cannot accommodate them.

ENCINO HOUSE EAST

Rent

412 Alvarado, SE

Albuquerque, NM 87108

(505) 266-7736

INDEPENDENT LIVING FACILITY

A residential apartment rental community for low-income and mature adults with disabilities. Another facility, called Encino House Midtown, is located on 609 Encino Place, NE in Albuquerque. Established in 1978 and sponsored by the New Mexico Conference of Churches.

HOUSING TYPES AVAILABLE

Studio and one-bedroom apartments in a five-story, two-wing building. Studios are 455 sq ft; one bedroom, 566 sq ft. There are 16 apartments for handicapped with 455 sq ft. All units are single level and open into wide hallways.

NUMBER OF SITES/UNITS

165 units.

LOCATION

Located near downtown Albuquerque in a somewhat marginal area directly next to a church and a post office. Security is emphasized; there is no easy outside access because of the nature of the building. The area itself is very convenient to hospitals (Lovelace Clinic is two miles away), doctors, shopping, churches, and entertainment.

REQUIREMENTS/RESTRICTIONS

Minimum age 62. Income and other federally mandated preferences to qualify.

FEES

Since this is a government-subsidized HUD Section 8 project, fees are determined based on income (the fee is 30 percent of a resident's income). When applying for residency, priority is given to persons meeting certain federal income and other mandated criteria. Rent includes all utilities except telephone, scheduled transportation, and use of community amenities. One meal a day (lunch) is served for which there is a $2 charge. Maid service is extra.

AMENITIES

Encino House has a lot to offer including a therapeutic pool, arts and crafts room, beauty shop, exercise room, and recreation area.

REVIEWER'S NOTES

This is an attractive community for low-income mature adults looking for a rental and wanting certain catered services. I was impressed with the people I met and with the community. There is a waiting list, and only people who meet federally mandated criteria are likely to be selected. If you are middle income you probably do not qualify. The average age of residents is 74.

LA VIDA LLENA RETIREMENT COMMUNITY

Buy

**10501 Lagrima
de Oro NE
Albuquerque, NM
87111
(505) 293-4001**

INDEPENDENT LIVING FACILITY

A lifecare community established in 1982 by the Lutheran, Presbyterian, Episcopalian, and Methodist churches of Albuquerque, members of which continue to serve on the board of directors.

HOUSING TYPES AVAILABLE

Apartments are located in a three-story building with indoor corridors. There are eight different floor plans to choose from. One studio floor plan is available with 385 sq ft and a small kitchenette. The one-bedroom model has 576 sq ft and a regular small kitchen. Six different two-bedroom models all have two baths and range in size from 798 to 1077 sq ft. The casita patio home has two bedrooms and two baths and is 1110 sq ft. The casitas have front and back yards and separate garages.

NUMBER OF SITES/UNITS

251 apartments, 8 casitas. More units are in the development stage.

LOCATION

Located in the northeast Heights area of Albuquerque, the community provides easy access to a hospital, physicians, shopping, and services. There is a good view of nearby mountains and Sandia Peak. This area is considered a good residential location.

REQUIREMENTS/RESTRICTIONS

Generally 62 years or older. There is an additional cost of 8 percent per year if you are under 62. Pets allowed only in casitas. Children may visit.

FEES

Entrance fees are based on apartment floor plan, and there are two plans (A and B) to choose between to structure your payment and equity. There is no deeded ownership, so make sure you fully understand both plans before you buy. Under Plan A, when you no longer can occupy your apartment, you or your estate will receive the entrance fee less 10 percent and less an additional one percent for each month you lived in the apartment. If you resided for five years in an apartment costing $80,000, the facility would retain a total of 70 percent ($56,000) of entrance fee and you would receive 30 percent. Plan B uses your age at the time of entrance to determine the entrance fee. With this plan, 94 percent is refundable. The same apartment that cost $80,000 under plan A will now cost a minimum of $108,000 (at age 62) or a maximum of $292,000 (age 95). If you lived there five years, the facility would keep 6 percent ($6480 to $17,520) and you would receive the 94 percent remaining. The entrance fees listed are those for purchase under Plan A and are based on single-person occupancy. Under Plan A, in all cases, add $12,000 to the initial fee for a second person. Plan B prices vary with age from $16,000 to $44,000. Studio price is $38,920 (only one occupant is permitted), and the one-bedroom model is $61,348. The prices for the six two-bedroom, two-bath units range from $80,220 to $104,972. The casita patio home is priced at $129,000. Monthly service fees are assessed by apartment size and will be listed for a single occupant. A second person is an additional $515 per month. The fee for a studio is $777; one bedroom, $911; and two-bedroom units, $1081 to $1317. Casitas are $1600. The fees include one meal per day, utilities, general maintenance, regular housekeeping, use of common areas, and facility security. Important to note, unlimited nursing care in La Vida Llena Health Care Center is covered in these fees under the residence agreement. Assisted living is also available in personal care suites.

AMENITIES

La Vida Llena has the broad range of amenities associated with good lifecare communities, including heated swimming pool, library, lounges, and crafts, billiard, and woodworking rooms. Scheduled transportation makes a private car unnecessary. Accessibility for the disabled is good; extra-wide hallways with handrails. Common areas and activity rooms are well appointed. Emergency call buttons are in all apartments.

REVIEWER'S NOTES

La Vida Llena is an example of an elegant southwestern lifecare community. The area nearby is residential and not congested. Additional units are being built, and there is currently a short waiting list to occupy certain models. The lifecare concept is attractive to many, and if you are interested in a relatively mild four-season climate this attractive facility merits further investigation.

Lake Powell Resorts & Marinas/ARA Leisure Services.

LAS COLINAS VILLAGE

Rent

500 Paisano NE

Albuquerque, NM 87123

(505) 291-0600

INDEPENDENT LIVING FACILITY

A rental community with a wide range of catered services. Established in 1985 by Dalworth Management and Realty of Fort Worth, which operates a number of retirement communities across the country.

HOUSING TYPES AVAILABLE

Six different floor plans are available. There are two studio models having 300 or 360 sq ft with mini-kitchens (no stove or oven). One-bedroom, one-bath models have equipped kitchens and are available with 559 or 614 sq ft. The two bedroom, one bath has 829 sq ft; and the two bedroom, two bath, 833 sq ft. Apartments are available on the first, second, and third floors. There is an elevator at the end of each floor and all hallways are enclosed.

NUMBER OF SITES/UNITS

130 apartments.

LOCATION

Las Colinas is located on Albuquerque's north side, a mainly residential section that includes many of the more expensive neighborhoods. A hospital is within five miles and branches of the renowned Lovelace Clinic are nearby. Shopping and churches are also within five miles. The airport is about 20 minutes away by car.

REQUIREMENTS/RESTRICTIONS

No minimum age requirements. Pets are allowed.

FEES

Monthly fees (single occupant) for apartments: studios, $825 and $875; one-bedroom units, $1125 and $1175; two-bedroom, one-bath units, $1375; and two bedroom, two bath, $1,450. A second occupant costs an additional $275 per month. These fees include three daily meals (it is possible to drop one meal per day for $60 off monthly fee), utilities, transportation seven days a week to any local destination, biweekly housekeeping, security cameras, emergency call buttons, scheduled activities, and the use of all common areas.

AMENITIES

Las Colinas offers many amenities in addition to those listed under fees. Apartments have wall-to-wall carpeting and cable TV hookups. Staff is on duty 24 hours a day. Especially noteworthy is the expanded transportation made available at all times to residents.

REVIEWER'S NOTES

Las Colinas Village offers a "catered" lifestyle to its residents. Buildings and grounds are pretty and well maintained. Its location is in a desirable neighborhood with mountain views. The low vacancy rate within this community could be taken as a recommendation. As there are very few of this type of rental/retirement communities in the Albuquerque area, Las Colinas should be contacted if you are interested in this type of rental situation.

MANZANO DEL SOL GOOD SAMARITAN RETIREMENT VILLAGE

Buy

5201 Roma Avenue, NE

Albuquerque, NM 87108

(505) 262-2311

INDEPENDENT LIVING FACILITY

An endowment retirement community offering independent living apartments and intermediate nursing care facilities. Established in 1980 by the Evangelical Lutheran Good Samaritan Society, a nonprofit organization. Headquartered in Sioux Falls, South Dakota, the Society operates 200 facilities nationwide.

HOUSING TYPES AVAILABLE

Apartments are available in three different floor plans. The smallest is a one-bedroom unit with 622 sq ft. Two-bedroom units have either 793 or 905 sq ft. The larger two-bedroom has two baths. The building has six stories with indoor hallways. Most apartments have balconies. There are 16 apartments specially adapted for disabled individuals.

NUMBER OF SITES/UNITS

156 apartments.

LOCATION

Manzano del Sol is conveniently located in the northeast area of Albuquerque. This area is very centrally located for services. Most points in the city are only 15 to 20 minutes away. Van transportation is provided for the residents Monday thru Friday.

REQUIREMENTS/RESTRICTIONS

Minimum age 55. Disabled persons may be eligible at age 50.

FEES

Entrance fee for the one-bedroom apartment is $20,000; two bedroom with one bath is $22,000; and the two bedroom, two bath is $25,000. The entrance fee is not refundable after five years of residence. During the first five years, if you should vacate your apartment, your entrance fee is amortized for the period during which you occupied the apartment. Monthly service fees are assessed as follows: $595 for one bedroom, $708 for two bedroom, and $833 for two bedroom, two bath. Utilities, monthly housekeeping, scheduled transportation, the use of recreational areas, and interior and exterior maintenance are included in this fee. Meals are not included but are served in the dining room. Breakfast is $2.50; lunch, $4.75; and dinner, $5.25. Meals may be purchased separately or with monthly tickets at a slightly reduced rate.

AMENITIES

Manzano del Sol offers a pool and Jacuzzi, craft rooms, a library, and a beauty and barber shop. Special assistance is available through homemaker aides. An emergency call button and daily "check-in" switch are provided in all apartments.

REVIEWER'S NOTES

Manzano del Sol is part of a large network of retirement facilities sponsored by the Good Samaritan group. The grounds and common areas are well kept and the central courtyard is very attractive. It seems difficult to get away from a rather institutional feeling in this reviewer's opinion. In view of the small number of vacancies, however, it would appear that the facility has appeal for retirees interested in an endowment facility.

THE MEADOWS MOBILE HOME COMMUNITY

7112 Pan American Freeway, NE

Albuquerque, NM 87109

(505) 821-1991

INDEPENDENT LIVING FACILITY

An adult mobile (manufactured) home community. Established in 1972 and owned by Meadows Realty, Newport Beach, CA.

HOUSING TYPES AVAILABLE

Mobile/manufactured preowned homes (single and double wide) with lots available. Prices range from $5500 to $35,500, depending on the model and lot selected. No new sales are available.

NUMBER OF SITES/UNITS

430 homes; 700 residents.

LOCATION

The Meadows is located just off I-25 in northeast Albuquerque. The area is excellent in terms of location, just a few minutes from hospitals (Northside is a few blocks away), doctors, shopping, churches, and entertainment. The area itself is a mix of residential properties, hotels, and some light industry. The Meadows is self-contained with one entrance and the area immediately nearby seems very safe.

REQUIREMENTS/RESTRICTIONS

55 and older; one small pet allowed.

FEES

Monthly rental for home sites ranges from $245 to $302 depending on size and location. Rent includes water, sewer, garbage, and the use of recreational facilities.

AMENITIES

The Meadows offers a central clubhouse/recreation center with a swimming pool, sauna, exercise room, library, and billiard room. There is an extensive program of planned activities. There is also protected RV parking.

REVIEWER'S NOTES

The Meadows is a very well-maintained and attractive mobile home community in a convenient location. I was impressed with the level of maintenance and appearance of the individual homes.

THE MONTEBELLO

Rent

10500 Academy Boulevard, NE Albuquerque, NM 87111 (505) 294-9944

INDEPENDENT LIVING FACILITY

A full-service rental community. Established in 1987; owned and operated by the Forum Group, Inc. of Indianapolis, which owns and operates communities nationwide.

HOUSING TYPES AVAILABLE

One- and two-bedroom apartments in a three-story complex. One-bedroom units range from 691 to 968 sq ft; two bedrooms, from 1027 to 1402 sq ft. All units are single level with seven floor plans to choose from. All except one model have patios or balconies. Apartments are attractive and open inward to a central corridor. All have emergency call buttons. Handicapped accessibility is adequate; wheelchairs and walkers are not allowed on a permanent basis. Attached to the community is a healthcare (nursing) facility with 15 beds for personal care and 60 beds for skilled nursing care.

NUMBER OF SITES/UNITS

114 apartments.

LOCATION

The Montebello is located in an exclusive area of northeast Albuquerque near the edge of the city. The area is attractive because it is upscale residential and one can avoid the congestion of the downtown areas while still being close to needed services. Hospitals, doctors' offices, shopping, churches, and entertainment are within five miles.

REQUIREMENTS/RESTRICTIONS

Minimum age 62. Pets are allowed.

FEES

One-bedroom apartments rent from $1645 to $1745 per month; two bedrooms, $2050 to $2150 depending on the floor chosen. There is a $315 a month additional person charge. These fees include one meal per day, all utilities, weekly maid service, transportation, 24-hour staff, and use of all amenities and services. A resident also earns 15 days of health care per year (a lifetime maximum of 60) for use if needed.

AMENITIES

The Montebello offers extensive catered services, including restaurant-style dining in an elegant dining room, 24-hour staffing for valet and emergency services, and a full-time recreation director who arranges the many social and recreational activities available. The community has an exercise room, a library, lounges, and craft and billiards rooms. There is no swimming pool.

REVIEWER'S NOTES

Montebello is an elegant rental community with a resort-type feeling. This is a good option for active people looking to rent and desiring catered or assisted living services combined with health care facilities.

EL CASTILLO RETIREMENT RESIDENCES

Buy

250 East Alameda

Santa Fe, NM 87501

(505) 988-2877

INDEPENDENT LIVING FACILITY

A lifecare community established in 1971 and owned and operated by a local not-for-profit community board.

HOUSING TYPES AVAILABLE

Studio, one-, and two-bedroom apartments available in three two-story buildings, each built around a courtyard. Studios are 400 sq ft, one bedrooms start at 600, and two bedrooms at 860. All are single level and open outward into a covered walkway. There are elevators for second-floor residents. The apartments are spacious with full kitchens and baths. Some have fireplaces. They were not built for disabled persons, but apparently some customization can be done.

NUMBER OF SITES/UNITS

114 apartments.

LOCATION

El Castillo is located on Alameda in the heart of downtown Santa Fe. The location is excellent for enjoying the sights and sounds of this unique small city. Hospitals, doctors, shopping, churches, and entertainment are all within a few miles—many within walking distance. El Castillo is built so that you enter across a small bridge into a main ample parking area. The three buildings and health care facility are spaciously set apart so you do not have a crowded feeling.

REQUIREMENTS/RESTRICTIONS

Minimum age 62. Pets not allowed.

FEES

This is a lifecare community in which residents pay an initial fee and then monthly fees in return for housing, assisted living services, other amenities, and nursing care guarantees for life. Initial fees range from $26,000 to $83,000; monthly fees range from $466 to $554. There is an additional person fee of $192 per month (for a second or third person). The monthly fee includes all utilities, scheduled transportation, one meal a day, housekeeping every other week, laundry services, and the use of community amenities and services. Initial fees are partially refundable if you decide to move based on the number of months of residence; there is no refund in case of death of the resident.

AMENITIES

The community offers a variety of amenities in addition to those mentioned above. There is an outdoor pool, an excellent library, recreation rooms, and, according to one of the residents, a significant number of social activities.

REVIEWER'S NOTES

El Castillo is an appealing lifecare community in an excellent downtown location. The facilities are older and do not have everything some newer developments offer, but they are well maintained and people seem to like living there. The residents we met were very positive about the community and the Santa Fe area.

PONCE DE LEON

Rent

640 Alta Vista

Santa Fe, NM 87501

(505) 984-8422; (800) 288-5678

INDEPENDENT LIVING FACILITY

An adult retirement apartment community providing a range of services for "catered" living. Established in 1986 by Ponce de Leon Limited Partnership and First Toledo Corporation, who retain ownership.

HOUSING TYPES AVAILABLE

Studio through two-bedroom, two-bath apartments in three-story elevator building. All apartments open to enclosed hallways and have either a patio or a balcony, depending on the floor. Studio apartments have approximately 450 sq ft; one bedroom, 550; and two bedroom, two bath, 835. All models have kitchens and walk-in closets. In addition to independent living apartments, there are apartments designated for assisted living.

NUMBER OF SITES/UNITS

150 apartments.

LOCATION

Ponce de Leon is located to the south and west of the historic downtown in central Santa Fe. The immediate surrounding area is a mixture of residential, commercial, and government buildings. The community is located across the street from a park, municipal pool, and tennis courts. Shopping and medical facilities are nearby. A special shuttle van is available for transportation to necessary locations as well as special destinations.

REQUIREMENTS/RESTRICTIONS

Although no specific age requirement exists, residents range in age from mid-50s to late 90s. The median age is in the seventies. Pets are permitted.

FEES

Studio apartments start at $1050 per month; one bedroom, $1210; and two bedroom, $1540. Rates are for one person; second person an additional $275 per month. The monthly fee includes lunch or dinner, utilities, a large lounge area with fireplace, recreation rooms, scheduled transportation, weekly housekeeping, flat linen service, cable TV, and varied activity program. Short-term furnished apartment rentals are also available at $1500 per month plus $300 second person monthly charge. Subtract $100 per person per month if meals are not desired.

AMENITIES

In addition to the amenities listed above, Ponce de Leon offers an elegant "Santa Fe-style" retirement. Interior common rooms have won design awards and are homey and comfortable. There is a central outdoor courtyard surrounded on all sides by apartments. The courtyard is landscaped and has a reflecting pool. There are emergency call switches in every apartment and a computerized "check-in" system for daily reassurance.

REVIEWER'S NOTES

Ponce de Leon appears to be exceptionally staffed with caring personnel. The facility is well maintained and quite lovely. While I would consider this gracious living, it does not seem pretentious. The residents' security and well-being appear to be of primary importance. Leasing agents were anxious to be accommodating. Santa Fe's four-season climate may not be for everyone, but if it appeals to you, this rental community should be contacted for more information.

GLOSSARY

Age restrictions Most if not all retirement communities have age restriction requirements. The Fair Housing Amendments Act of 1988 prohibits or complicates many of these requirements. So this is an unclear area at the moment. Proposals are currently in Congress to eliminate the impact of the 1988 act on retirement communities.

Assisted living Same feature as catered community, but with additional medical/nursing or nurses' aide services.

Catered community Features full custodial service covered by rent or service fees. Services usually include meals, transportation, and housekeeping.

Condominium Commonly used to describe apartment-style multi-family dwellings.

Congregate care Same as catered community but typically a term stressing common services in a community setting. Almost always implies shared dining, transportation, housekeeping services, and certain medical services on the premises.

Continuing Care Retirement Community A term used by some to mean a Lifecare Community. The more common use is to describe a community with several levels of retirement living from independent living to licensed nursing care.

Desert landscaping Designed around gravel/rock and cactus or other desert plants. Popular; requires less maintenance than grass.

Duplexes In Southwest, two homes sharing one common wall.

Endowment A community where an initial endowment (entrance fee) is required and often partially refundable based on certain formulas and resale of the unit. The fee probably does not cover nursing home costs.

Garden villa A home attached to one or more similar units, usually with a garden or patio.

HUD subsidized housing A government program which provides subsidized rental housing to low-income elderly and/or disabled persons.

Lifecare A community in which a resident pays an initial endowment or entrance fee and then monthly fees and in return receives housing and nursing care for life. There are a variety of formulas, which include the return of a portion or all of the initial fee depending on certain conditions. Other key provisions involve guarantees made by the community to the resident. Not all communities provide nursing care for life.

Patio home In most cases, a townhouse or condominium with a private landscaped patio. Sometimes refers to a smaller single-family home on a smaller lot.

Planned community Developed by a single developer or corporation to provide houses that are architecturally harmonious, with preplanned amenities and features.

Prefabricated home Manufactured in a factory and assembled on the owner's lot. Once set up it is difficult to move.

Recreation center or club house (interchangeable) Refers to a common facility or area available to all residents in the community.

RV (Recreational Vehicle) In this publication, a motorhome or travel trailer.

Single-family home Freestanding home with no shared wall with another unit.

Snowbirds Locals' name for winter visitors.

Townhome Same as condominium.

INDEX BY COMMUNITY TYPE

Westchester Villa, Tempe, AZ
Westminister Village, Scottsdale, AZ
Whispering Pines of Mesa, Mesa, AZ
Wooddale Village, Sun City, AZ

CONDOMINIUM/ TOWNHOUSE APARTMENTS

Ahwatukee, Phoenix, AZ
Broadway Proper, Tucson, AZ
CAMLU, Albuquerque, NM
CAMLU, Las Vegas, NV
CAMLU, Tucson, AZ
Campana del Rio, Tucson, AZ
Casa del Rio, Peoria, AZ
The Cascades, Tucson, AZ
Chandler Villas, Chandler, AZ
Cheyenne Retirement Campus, North Las Vegas, NV
Colter Village, Glendale, AZ
Cottonwood Village, Cottonwood, AZ
Del Webb's Sun City Las Vegas, Las Vegas, NV
Desert Amethyst, Peoria, AZ
El Castillo, Santa Fe, NM
El Dorado, Sun City, AZ
Encino House East, Albuquerque, NM
Fairfield's La Cholla Hills, Tucson, AZ
Fellowship Square, Phoenix, AZ
The Fountains at La Cholla, Tucson, AZ
Friendship Village of Tempe, Tempe, AZ
Glencroft, Glendale, AZ
Glencroft—North, Phoenix, AZ
Green Valley, Green Valley, AZ
Greenfields, Glendale, AZ
La Vida Llena, Albuquerque, NM

Las Colinas Village, Albuquerque, NM
Leisure World, Mesa, AZ
Madison House, Sun City West, AZ
Manzano del Sol, Albuquerque, NM
Montara Meadows, Las Vegas, NV
The Montebello, Albuquerque, NM
Olive Grove Retirement Village, Phoenix, AZ
Orangewood, Phoenix, AZ
The Orchard, Mesa, AZ
Paradise Cove, Las Vegas, NV
Paradise Valley Estates, Phoenix, AZ
Phoenix Manor, Phoenix, AZ
Phoenix Mountain Villa, Phoenix, AZ
Ponce de Leon, Santa Fe, NM
Royal Oaks, Sun City, AZ
Royal Palms, Mesa, AZ
Ryerson Heritage, Sun City, AZ
Santa Catalina Villas, Tucson, AZ
Scottsdale Shadows, Scottsdale, AZ
Scottsdale Village Square, Scottsdale, AZ
The Springs of North Mesa, Mesa, AZ
The Springs of Scottsdale, Scottsdale, AZ
Sun City, Sun City, AZ
Sun City Tucson, Tucson, AZ
Sun City West, Sun City West, AZ
Sun Grove, Peoria, AZ
Sun Village, Surprise, AZ
Sunland Village East, Mesa, AZ
Thunderbird Gardens, Glendale, AZ

Villa Ocotillo, Scottsdale, AZ
The Village at Apache Wells, Mesa, AZ
Westbrook Village, Peoria, AZ
Westchester Villa, Tempe, AZ
Westminster Village, Scottsdale, AZ
Whispering Pines of Mesa, Mesa, AZ
Wooddale Village, Sun City, AZ

GOLF

Ahwatukee, Phoenix, AZ
Apache Wells, Mesa, AZ
Del Webb's Sun City Las Vegas, Las Vegas, NV
Dreamland Villa, Mesa, AZ
El Dorado, Sun City, AZ
Friendly Village of Orangewood, Phoenix, AZ
Green Valley, Green Valley, AZ
Happy Trails, Surprise, AZ
Leisure World
Paradise Peak West, Phoenix, AZ
Riverview RV Resort,
Royal Palms Retirement, Mesa, AZ
SaddleBrooke, Tucson, AZ
Scottsdale Shadows, Scottsdale, AZ
Snowbird RV Resort, Bullhead City, AZ
Sun City, Sun City, AZ
Sun City Tucson, Tucson, AZ
Sun City West, Sun City West, AZ
Sun Lakes, Sun Lakes, AZ
Sun Village, Surprise, AZ
Sunland Village East, Mesa, AZ
Westbrook Village, Peoria, AZ

LIFECARE/ENDOWMENT

All lifecare facilities have care facilities

El Castillo (LC), Santa Fe, NM

The Forum-Pueblo Norte (LC), Scottsdale, AZ

Friendship Village of Tempe (LC), Tempe, AZ

Glencroft (EN), Glendale, AZ

Glencroft-North (EN), Phoenix, AZ

La Vida Llena (LC), Albuquerque, NM

Manzano del Sol (EN), Albuquerque, NM

Orangewood (EN), Phoenix, AZ

Paradise Valley Estates (EN), Phoenix, AZ

Royal Oaks (LC), Sun City, AZ

Westminster Village (LC), Scottsdale, AZ

MOBILE/MANUFACTURED HOMES

Apache Wells, Mesa, AZ

Boulder Ridge, Phoenix, AZ

Casa del Sol #1, Peoria, AZ

Casa del Sol #2, Glendale, AZ

Casa del Sol #3, Peoria, AZ

Friendly Village of Orangewood, Phoenix, AZ

Happy Trails, Surprise, AZ

Kingman Ranch, Kingman, AZ

The Meadows, Las Vegas, NV

The Meadows Mobile Home Community, Albuquerque, NM

Palm Gardens Mobile Home Manor, Mesa, AZ

Paradise Peak West, Phoenix, AZ

Phoenix North Mobile Home Community, Phoenix, AZ

Sunrise Vista, Mesa, AZ

Swan Lake Estates, Tucson, AZ

Three Crowns Mobile Manor, Las Vegas, NV

Trails West, Tucson, AZ

Villa Borega, Las Vegas, NV

The Wells at Red Mountain, Mesa, AZ

RENTAL

Broadway Proper, Tucson, AZ

CAMLU, Albuqureque, NM

CAMLU, Las Vegas, NV

CAMLU, Tucson, AZ

Campana del Rio, Tucson, AZ

Casa del Rio, Peoria, AZ

The Cascades, Tucson, AZ

Chandler Villas, Chandler, AZ

Cheyenne Retirement Campus, North Las Vegas, NV

Colter Village, Glendale, AZ

Cottonwood Village, Cottonwood, AZ

Desert Amethyst, Peoria, AZ

Encino House East, Albuquerque, NM

Fellowship Square, Phoenix, AZ

The Fountains at La Cholla, Tucson, AZ

Greenfields, Glendale, AZ

Las Colinas Village, Albuquerque, NM

Madison House, Sun City West, AZ

Montara Meadows, Las Vegas, NV

Olive Grove Retirement Village, Phoenix, AZ

The Orchard, Mesa, AZ

Paradise Cove, Las Vegas, NV

Phoenix Manor, Phoenix, AZ

Phoenix Mountain Villa, Phoenix, AZ

Ponce de Leon, Santa Fe, NM

Royal Palms, Mesa, AZ

Santa Catalina Villas, Tucson, AZ

Scottsdale Village Square, Scottsdale, AZ

The Springs of North Mesa, Mesa, AZ

The Springs of Scottsdale, Scottsdale, AZ

Sun Grove Resort Village, Peoria, AZ

Thunderbird Gardens, Glendale, AZ

Villa Ocotillo, Scottsdale, AZ

The Village at Apache Wells, Mesa, AZ

Westchester Villa, Tempe, AZ

Whispering Pines of Mesa, Mesa, AZ

Wooddale Village, Sun City, AZ

RV (See also area reviews of Quartzsite and Yuma)

Good Life RV Resort, Mesa, AZ

Greenfield Village RV Resort, Mesa, AZ

Happy Trails, Surprise, AZ

Mesa Regal RV Resort, Mesa, AZ

Palm Gardens Mobile Home Manor, Mesa, AZ

Rincon Country East and West, Tucson, AZ

Riverview RV Resort, Bullhead City, AZ

Snowbird RV Resort, Bullhead City, AZ

Sunflower Resort, Surprise, AZ

View Point RV Resort, Mesa, AZ

Voyager, Tucson, AZ

SINGLE FAMILY HOMES

Ahwatukee, Phoenix, AZ
Apache Wells, Mesa, AZ
Del Webb's Sun City Las Vegas,
    Las Vegas, NV
Dreamland Villa, Mesa, AZ
Fairfield's La Cholla Hills,
    Tucson, AZ
Friendship Village of Tempe,
    Tempe, AZ
Green Valley, Green Valley, AZ
La Cholla Hills, Tucson, AZ
Leisure World
SaddleBrooke, Tucson, AZ
Sun City, Sun City, AZ
Sun City Tucson, Tucson, AZ
Sun City West, Sun City West,
    AZ
Sun Lakes, Sun Lakes, AZ
Sun Village, Surprise, AZ
Sunland Village East, Mesa, AZ

Westbrook Village, Peoria, AZ

WINTER VISITORS (See also Quartzsite area review)

Casa del Rio, Peoria, AZ
Chandler Villas, Chandler, AZ
Del Webb's Sun City Las Vegas,
    Las Vegas, NV
Good Life RV Resort, Mesa, AZ
Greenfield Village RV Resort,
    Mesa, AZ
Greenfields, Glendale, AZ
Happy Trails, Surprise, AZ
Madison House, Sun City West,
    AZ
Mesa Regal RV Resort, Mesa, AZ
Palm Gardens Mobile Home
    Manor, Mesa, AZ
Paradise Cove, Las Vegas, NV
Ponce de Leon, Santa Fe, NM

Rincon Country East and West,
    Tucson, AZ
Riverview RV Resort, Bullhead
    City, AZ
Royal Palms, Mesa, AZ
Santa Catalina Villas, Tucson, AZ
Scottsdale Shadows, Scottsdale,
    AZ
Snowbird RV Resort, Bullhead
    City, AZ
The Springs of North Mesa,
    Mesa, AZ
Sun City, Sun City, AZ
Sun City Tucson, Tucson, AZ
Sun City West, Sun City, AZ
Sunflower Resort, Surprise, AZ
Thunderbird Gardens, Glendale,
    AZ
View Point RV Resort, Mesa, AZ
Voyager, Tucson, AZ
Whispering Pines of Mesa,
    Mesa, AZ